Active Experiences for Active Children

LITERACY EMERGES

Carol Seefeldt
Alice Galper

Merrill
Prentice Hall

Upper Saddle River, New Jersey
Columbus, Ohio

Library of Congress Cataloging in Publication Data

Seefeldt, Carol.
   Active experiences for active children / Carol Seefeldt, Alice Galper.
     p. cm.
   Includes bibliographical references and index.
   ISBN 0-13-083435-1 (pbk.)
   1. Language arts (Early childhood) 2. Active learning. I. Galper, Alice. II. Title.

LB1139.5.L35 S44 2001
372.6'044—dc21
                                             00-061615

Vice President and Publisher: Jeffery W. Johnston
Executive Editor: Ann Castel Davis
Editorial Assistant: Pat Grogg
Production Editor: Sheryl Glicker Langner
Design Coordinator: Diane C. Lorenzo
Photo Coordinator: Nancy Harre Ritz
Cover Designer: Ceri Fitzgerald
Cover Photo: FPG
Production Manager: Laura Messerly
Director of Marketing: Kevin Flanagan
Marketing Manager: Amy June
Marketing Services Manager: Krista Groshong

This book was set in Times and Frutiger by Carlisle Communications, Ltd. It was printed and bound by Courier Kendallville, Inc. The cover was printed by Phoenix Color Corp.

Photo Credits: pp. 3, 41, 55, 67 by Anne Vega/Merrill; pp. 8, 36, 46, 109 by Todd Yarrington/Merrill; pp. 15, 31 by Barbara Schwartz/Merrill; pp. 19, 81, 95, 121, 135 by Anthony Magnacca/Merrill; p. 147 by Scott Cunningham/Merrill.

1 0 9 8 7 6 5 4 3 2
ISBN: 0-13-083435-1

◆ This book is dedicated to Ann Davis, editor extraordinaire.

Preface

"What can I do tomorrow?" teachers ask. "And I don't mean just another silly activity. I need something that will keep children involved and lead to successful learning." Grounded in John Dewey's philosophy that all genuine education comes through experience, but that not all experiences are equally educative, *Active Experiences for Active Children: Literacy Emerges* answers teachers' questions about what to do tomorrow.

Both pre- and in-service teachers will find this book useful. It is suitable as a text, or a supplemental text, for early childhood courses in community colleges and four-year college programs.

There are numerous activity books available. These, however, present isolated language activities that are often meaningless to children and void of any real content or learning. *Active Experiences for Active Children: Literacy Emerges* offers teachers an integrated approach to planning language learning for young children.

Its practicality will also be ideal for teachers who desire the best for young children but have limited training or formal preparation. Professionals working in childcare, Head Start, or other early childhood settings will find that *Active Experiences for Active Children: Literacy Emerges* supports their growth and understanding of how to put theory into practice.

ORGANIZATION

This book is the second in a series of books designed to illustrate how to plan and implement meaningful, thematic experiences that truly educate young children instead of just keeping them busy. Teachers are given guides to planning and implementing curriculum that will lead to children's academic success.

Active Experiences for Active Children: Literacy Emerges consists of clear, concise, and usable guides for planning meaningful language learning experiences for children in childcare, preschool, Head Start, or other early educational programs.

The experiences in this book lead to successful language learning because they

- are grounded on children's interests and needs and in their here-and-now world

- have integrity in terms of content key to language learning and learning to read and write

- involve children in group work and projects

- have continuity. One experience builds on another, forming a complete, coherent, integrated learning curriculum for young children as well as connecting the early childhood setting to children's homes and communities.

- promote the language skills and attitudes children will need not only to perpetuate our democratic society, but to continually improve that society

- provide time and opportunity for children to think and reflect on their experiences

The first four chapters describe how to plan and implement experiential language learning. These offer pre- and in-service teachers of young children an overview of theory and research on the role of experiences in children's language learning. The first chapter illustrates how Dewey's theories of learning and teaching can be put into practice. This is followed by chapters on the role of language learning environments, in the classroom, home, and community. Chapter 4 reviews research and theory and discusses concepts key to language learning, reading and writing.

Next, eight guides for planning and implementing active and meaningful language experiences are presented. These guides include sections for the teacher and for the children.

The section "For the Teacher" begins by identifying concepts key to learning language, reading, and writing. Goals and objectives are stated. This section discusses ideas for connecting children's home and family to the school, and describes how to evaluate and assess children's language learning.

The section "For the Children" consists of ideas for implementing the identified goals and objectives through thematic, integrated, and continual experiences. In this case, the guides are based on skills and knowledge required for literacy to emerge.

AUTHORS

Another important feature of the book is the expertise and background of the authors. Together, they bring a unique perspective to the book. Both have experienced Deweyan education. Both have worked in Head Start, childcare, and other early childhood settings and thus bring an intimate knowledge of practice to the text. And because both are researchers, the latest in theory and research in the field of early childhood education is represented in the text.

ACKNOWLEDGMENTS

We wish to thank Ann Davis, whose knowledge of active children and thoughtful guidance contributed to the development of this book. We appreciate the expertise of Sheryl Langner. The careful attention of Pat Grogg to the details of book production merits special thanks.

We would like to thank the following for their valuable suggestions and comments: Adrienne L. Herrell, California State University, Fresno; Alice S. Honig, Syracuse University; Leanna Manna, Villa Maria College (NY); Edythe H. Schwartz, California State University, Sacramento; and Thomas D. Yawkey, Penn State University.

Discover the Companion Website Accompanying This Book

THE PRENTICE HALL COMPANION WEBSITE: A VIRTUAL LEARNING ENVIRONMENT

Technology is a constantly growing and changing aspect of our field that is creating a need for content and resources. To address this emerging need, Prentice Hall has developed an online learning environment for students and professors alike—Companion Websites—to support our textbooks.

In creating a Companion Website, our goal is to build on and enhance what the textbook already offers. For this reason, the content for each user-friendly website is organized by topic and provides the professor and student with a variety of meaningful resources. Common features of a Companion Website include:

FOR THE PROFESSOR—

Every Companion Website integrates **Syllabus Manager™,** an online syllabus creation and management utility.

- **Syllabus Manager™** provides you, the instructor, with an easy, step-by-step process to create and revise syllabi, with direct links into Companion Website and other online content without having to learn HTML.

- Students may logon to your syllabus during any study session. All they need to know is the web address for the Companion Website and the password you've assigned to your syllabus.

- After you have created a syllabus using **Syllabus Manager™,** students may enter the syllabus for their course section from any point in the Companion Website.

- Class dates are highlighted in white and assignment due dates appear in blue. Clicking on a date, the student is shown the list of activities for the assignment. The activities for each assignment are linked directly to actual content, saving time for students.

- Adding assignments consists of clicking on the desired due date, then filling in the details of the assignment—name of the assignment, instructions, and whether or not it is a one-time or repeating assignment.

- In addition, links to other activities can be created easily. If the activity is online, a URL can be entered in the space provided, and it will be linked automatically in the final syllabus.

- Your completed syllabus is hosted on our servers, allowing convenient updates from any computer on the Internet. Changes you make to your syllabus are immediately available to your students at their next logon.

FOR THE STUDENT—

- **Topic Overviews**—outline key concepts in topic areas

- **Electronic Bluebook**—send homework or essays directly to ˌ ̖ ̖ instructor's email with this paperless form

- **Message Board**—serves as a virtual bulletin board to post—or res̖ questions or comments to/from a national audience

- **Web Destinations**—links to www sites that relate to each topic area

- **Professional Organizations**—links to organizations that relate to topic areas

- **Additional Resources**—access to topic-specific content that enhances material found in the text

To take advantage of these and other resources, please visit the *Active Experiences for Active Children: Literacy Emerges* Companion Website at

www.prenhall.com/seefeldt

About the Authors

Carol Seefeldt, Ph.D., is Professor Emeritus of human development at the Institute for Child Study, University of Maryland, College Park, where she taught graduate and undergraduate classes for 28 years. She received the Distinguished Scholar-Teacher Award from the university and has published 23 books and over 100 scholarly and research articles for teachers and parents. Her books include *Social Studies for the Preschool/Primary Child, Active Experiences for Active Children: Social Studies,* and *Current Issues in Early Childhood Education* with Alice Galper, and *The Early Childhood Curriculum: Current Findings in Theory and Practice.*

During her 40 years in the field, Dr. Seefeldt has taught at every level from nursery school for 2-year-olds through the third grade. In Florida she directed a church-related kindergarten, and served as Regional Training Officer for Project Head Start. She has conducted teacher training programs in Japan and the Ukraine and has been a frequent guest on radio and television talk shows.

Carol's research interests have revolved around curriculum development and program evaluation as well as intergenerational attitudes. Most recently she was principal investigator of the Montgomery County Head Star—Public School Transition Demonstration.

Alice Galper, Ph.D., educator and consultant, received her doctorate from the University of Maryland, College Park. Previously she was a classroom teacher in New Hampshire and a Head Start Consultant in the Washington, DC, area. She was a professor of human development teaching graduate and undergraduate courses in early childhood and human development at Mt. Vernon College, Washington, DC, for nearly 20 years and at the University of Maryland. She assisted Carol Seefeldt on the research component of the Montgomery County Head Start—Public School Transition Demonstration. Currently she is on the adjunct faculty at the University of Maryland.

Alice's research has revolved around intergenerational attitudes and program evaluation. She has written many articles for such journals as *Child Development, Journal of Educational Psychology,* and *Early Childhood Research Quarterly.* She is co-author with Carol Seefeldt of *Continuing Issues in Early Childhood Education* and *Active Experiences for Active Children: Social Studies.*

Alice presents workshops and papers regularly at the National Association for the Education of Young Children Conference, the Head Start Research Conference, and the Society for Research in Child Development Biennial Meetings, among others.

Active in community affairs, Alice has been appointed by Mayor Anthony Williams of Washington, DC, as co-chair of the Interagency Coordinating Council of the DC Early Intervention Program for Infants and Toddlers, and volunteers for the Black Student Fund.

Contents

Building Connections to Home and Community: Extending Active Literacy Experiences   31

The Form and Structure of Language Learning   41

PART TWO
Guides to Active Experiences   53

7 Writing Throughout the Day: Using Invented Spelling   135

8 Second Language Learners: English as a Second Language   147

PART ONE

Theory of Active Experiences

1

Experiences and Language Learning
Theory Into Practice

All genuine education comes about through experience . . . but not all experiences are genuinely or equally educative.

John Dewey, 1938, p. 13

Active Experiences for Active Children—Literacy Emerges guides teachers of 3- to 5-year-old children in planning and implementing meaningful learning experiences designed to foster literacy development and skills in children in childcare settings, nursery schools and preschools, Head Start, and kindergartens. The book is based on the idea that literacy emerges from integrated, meaningful experiences that occur within the social context of the classroom rather than from drill and practice activities.

According to Dewey's philosophy of education, language learning takes place not as a series of lessons or drills in isolated skills but as a social necessity. Vygotsky (1986), as well, believed language learning, in every culture, takes place through everyday interactions and shared experiences between adult and child. Obviously in different cultures the interactions and words differ, but the process remains remarkably similar (Chomsky, 1986).

As a mother dresses her toddler, she talks about what they are doing: "Put your arm here, in this sleeve. Now the other arm." "Here is your hat," she says as she puts it on the child's head. The sounds "hat," "sleeve," and "arm," when repeated as mother and child share many different and varied experiences with the objects, soon come to have the same meaning for mother and child (Moore, Angelopoulos, & Bennett, 1999; Whitehurst & Lonigan, 1998). After a while the child understands that the word "hat" stands for the thing on her head. Then she can find her hat when her mother asks, "Where's your hat?" And she can use the word "hat" to communicate her ideas of hats to others.

According to the joint position paper of the National Association for the Education of Young Children and the International Reading Association (NAEYC & IRA, 1998), language learning takes place in much the same way when children are in childcare, preschool, kindergarten, or other early childhood settings. A curriculum built around shared, meaningful experiences has many of the same characteristics and the same social necessity as the common, everyday interactions between parent and child.

In schools for young children, language and experiences go together. You cannot have one without the other. Experiences demand *listening, speaking, writing, and reading.* Experiences give children something in common to *talk* about. Probably every child in our country has been to a supermarket. But when children go as a group for a specific purpose, they see the store differently. Because they share the same experience, they have a foundation for communicating with one another. From the common experience of going to a supermarket or some other place in the community or school, themes for sociodramatic play, murals, and other group projects emerge. These, in turn, give children still more to talk about, listen to, and express through play, drawing, painting, and writing.

Language is made necessary. Before taking a trip, children discuss the trip they are about to take. They talk about the purposes of the trip, what they think they will see and do. Their questions are listed on a chart in English and, when possible, in the children's home languages. In preparation for the trip, the chart is cut apart, and each child, or small group of children, is given one of the questions to ask while on the trip. A letter is written to the people they will be visiting. Following the trip, children will need to write a thank-you letter to the same people, and express their ideas and feelings through drawing, writing, constructing, and painting.

Children consult and read books. Depending on children's needs, these could include reference books, picture dictionaries, and picture books and storybooks, both factual and fiction. Bilingual picture books and dictionaries, or those written in children's home languages, are available to the children. Books are found not just in the library area, but also in the housekeeping area, near the blocks, or in the science and mathematics areas.

When teachers plan and implement meaningful experiences such as a trip to the supermarket, local garage, or clothing store, they are providing children with the opportunity to

- learn new vocabulary through firsthand experiences that result in gaining a store of concepts,

- learn language within a social context through interaction with others,

- bring meaning to the form and structure of language, and

- learn to think about and reflect on their experiences.

LEARN NEW VOCABULARY

New vocabulary seems best learned within the context of meaningful experiences (Adams, 1998). This seems especially true for children who are new to the United States and just beginning to learn English, as well as for those who are language delayed, or speech or hearing impaired, or who have some other special need (Garcia, 1996; Gonzalez, 1996; NAEYC, 1996). Meaningful experiences that lead to language learning are *firsthand,* are *initiated* by the children, and are *continuous.*

Firsthand Experiences

Active Experiences for Active Children—Literacy Emerges involves children in firsthand experiences. Basing children's learning on content that can be experienced *firsthand* guarantees a measure of meaning. Children are not asked to learn vocabulary or the form and structure of language secondhand by listening to someone else recite the alphabet or tell them about nouns, verbs, adjectives, or adverbs.

Rather, children learn language when they are involved in touching, taking apart, tasting, and smelling things in their here-and-now world. By doing so, they are the ones who receive information and learn vocabulary and the form and structure of language firsthand. And because their experiences are firsthand, they are the ones who can use the experiences to make sense of their world and to form ideas and concepts. These concepts, in turn, spur the learning of new words. And the new words, in turn, shape children's concepts, enabling them to extend and refine their ideas of the world (Vygotsky, 1986).

Piaget's work fully documented that active, firsthand experiences are necessary if children are to learn language, to think, and to construct knowledge (Piaget & Inhelder, 1969). Vygotsky (1978) saw this convergence of speech and physical activity as a necessary step in language learning.

Active children engaged in firsthand experiences are full of language. They talk, sing, and chant as they play house, paint, build with blocks, or create a sculpture out of boxes. Their speech and physical activity merge. Further, the more linguistically and culturally diverse a group, the more critical it is for learners to be active, engaged in hands-on interactive experiences that allow them to explore ideas of significance to their lives (Garcia, 1996).

When children are actually involved in meaningful experiences, the necessity for naming and describing things in their world becomes real. An experience in a linguistically diverse Head Start class illustrates this. In this class, nearly half of the children spoke Spanish, one spoke Russian, and two others Chinese. To foster language learning for all the children, the teacher brought a number of swallowtail chrysalises to class. She told children the name of the hard-shelled pupa was *chrysalis,* and wrote the word in Spanish, English, and Russian as she said it in each language. When the butterflies emerged, she did the same with the word *emerge.* Together the children and teacher looked through books about butterflies to identify their butterflies and learned they were swallowtails. The children painted a mural of the butterflies. One told a visitor, "We watched the most beautiful swallowtails emerge from their chrysalises, and then we painted all the beautiful butterflies."

Initiative, Choices, and Decision Making

When children can take the *initiative* and make choices and decisions about the activities they will engage in, language learning is fostered. Taking the initiative, children are the ones who use language to help them organize the activities they have chosen, and who use words to plan what to do and how to do it.

The bulk of their language learning will take place as children work in centers of interest both indoors and outdoors. But making choices and taking the initiative occur not just through interacting with others during center time. Real problems that arise from living together give children the opportunity to take the initiative. This helps make the use of language a necessity to solve problems and control themselves and others (Dewey, 1944; Vygotsky, 1978).

In one childcare center, a group of 3-year-olds seemed unable to take part in clean-up time. After one particularly difficult and chaotic clean-up period, the teacher gathered the 3-year-olds around her and asked, "What happened?" One child replied, "We ran and threw things." Another said, "It was a mess." "Yes," the teacher agreed, "but what are we going to do about it? We must clean up so we can have lunch." One child, taking the initiative, said, "I'll put the dolls in the house," and another added, "Casey and me will put the blocks away." Others chimed in and together put the room back in order.

In another center, Calan was observed putting blocks away by himself as the others listened to a story. When asked why he was not listening to the story with the others, he replied, "It's logical consequences." When asked what logical consequences were, he said, "You see, I did not put the blocks away during clean-up time, so the logical consequences are I have to put them away now."

Both of these situations demonstrate that children, even very young ones, can learn and use complex vocabulary when this language is presented to them in a meaningful context. In both situations, children used language as a means of understanding, thinking, and solving problems (Vygotsky, 1978).

Continuous Experiences

If children are to gain vocabulary, they must encounter the words they hear and experience them over and over again in a variety of contexts. So teachers plan such additional experiences. They may take children to visit a local construction site and introduce the vocabulary of building. They then reintroduce this vocabulary in connection with children's block building. Books, poems, and other literature using the same vocabulary and language are read, continually reinforcing children's language learning.

When experiences are continuous, children have the time and opportunity to see relationships between facts; to develop ideas, generalize, and extrapolate; to make a tentative intuitive leap into new knowledge. This leap, from merely learning a fact to connecting one fact to another, is an essential step in concept formation (Bruner, 1966).

Just as experiences serve to connect children's thinking, so can they serve to unite home and school. Connecting home and school is especially necessary when children and their families speak a language other than English. "Educational programs and families must respect and reinforce each other as they work together to achieve the greatest benefit for all children" (Neuman et al., 1999, p. 184). This means educators must accept the legitimacy of children's home languages, respect and value the home culture, and promote and encourage the active involvement and support of all families. This book demonstrates how to do that. Each experience specifies a role for children's families, enabling them to become active partners with teachers in developing children's literacy skills and knowledge.

GAIN A STORE OF CONCEPTS

Through shared experiences, the child comes to know that the sound of "hat" stands for the thing on her head. But then she encounters the sound, and it refers to the thing on her father's head, which looks quite different from her own hat. A neighbor visits who has another kind of hat on her head. Eventually the word "hat" comes to stand for a whole group of hats, not just the unique one on the child's head, and now the child has constructed an idea or a concept of "hat."

Concepts are the ingredients of thinking. Without conceptual understanding, children might be able to sound out the word "hat"—"h/ ae/ t/"—but would have no understanding that these sounds stand for the idea of hat. Without this conceptual understanding, children cannot gain meaning from either the spoken or written word (Whitehurst & Lonigian, 1998).

With enough drill and practice and perhaps a lot of reinforcement, children can memorize a great many facts. Unfortunately, children who are taught only through drill and practice are rather like parrots that have been taught to recite a poem or sing a song. Neither parrots nor children have any idea or concept of what has been memorized.

Further, facts are not concepts. Children must be able to see the relationships between isolated facts and make generalizations. The child learning the word "hat" must be able to relate her hat to other hats she sees and hears named, and to reach the generalization that even though hats differ, they are alike in the fact that they all are used to cover heads. This conceptualization is necessary to bring meaning to the spoken and printed word.

Through handling objects and observing things in their world, children begin to connect isolated facts and make generalizations. They compare, classify, and sequence objects and things: "All of these are fruits." Children relate new information to their existing ideas or concepts of how the world works, fitting it into their schemes, or ideas. Three-year-old Andrea, familiar with eating an apple by biting into it, was given an orange. Assimilating the new fruit into her existing idea of fruit, she bit into the orange. When she found this didn't work, that the orange did not fit her existing concept or idea of fruit, she had to change her idea, and create a new one—some fruits need to be peeled before eating. Many firsthand experiences and encounters with their world are necessary for children to construct, as Andrea did, their own knowledge of the world and store it as concepts, rules, or principles (Piaget & Inhelder, 1969).

All these are the same—beginning concept formation.

Children's first concepts are embryonic in nature. These early concepts "stand in the same relationship to true concepts as the embryo to the full formed organism" (Vygotsky, 1986, p. 58). Although inaccurate, incomplete, and vague, children's early concepts are sufficient to permit them to make simple classifications of the things in their world and bring meaning to the spoken and written language.

Experts from nearly every subject area have identified concepts key to their disciplines. These organized concepts direct and guide curriculum planning for young children. Concepts key to language learning and its form and structure have been identified by the National Association for the Education of Young Children and the International Reading Association (1998). These concepts form the foundation for the experiences in this book.

INTERACT WITH OTHERS—THE SOCIAL CONTEXT OF LANGUAGE LEARNING

Interacting with the physical environment is not the only prerequisite for language learning. Children must also interact with their peers, teachers, and other adults if they are to have true experiences that lead to language learning. For all children, but especially those whose home language is other than English, both adults and peers are sources of information and serve as sounding boards against which children can test the accuracy of their language, thinking, and knowledge (Clay, 1979; Gambrells & Mazzoni, 1999; Genishi & Fassler 1999; Maryland State Department of Education [MSDE],

1992). Therefore, all of the experiences in this book involve children in *play,* in *group work and projects,* and in *interactions with teachers and other adults.*

Play

Children need the time and opportunity for *play,* especially for sociodramatic play, which requires other children. Both Vygotsky (1978) and Piaget (Piaget & Inhelder, 1969) believed this type of play led to language use and symbolic thought. When children play "as if" they were the mother, baby, father, or teacher and "as if" a block were a scissors, they are thinking abstractly. Not only are they using objects to symbolize something not present, a skill critical to learning to read, but they are convincing each other, using language, that the block is a scissors.

Other types of play—play with board games, building with blocks, play with puzzles and other small manipulatives—foster children's visual discrimination, give them practice in making such discriminations. Playing with pegboards and parquet blocks, children must observe the characteristics of the materials, make visual discriminations, sort, classify, and predict how the materials will work. Development of visual discrimination leads children to later being able to discriminate between and among letters. By sorting, classifying, and ordering the manipulatives, children gain skills necessary for both concept and language learning.

There is even a role for language in rough-and-tumble physical play, including arguments and fighting. Piaget and Inhelder (1969) saw value in children's arguments. When children argue and disagree with one another, they must bump their ideas of the situation head-on into the ideas of others. In doing so, they have to rethink their view of the way things are, adjust their thinking, and find the words to convince others that their way of thinking is the most preferable.

Research also points out that children only learn vocabulary and concepts of in and out, up and down, and other directional concepts by experiencing themselves climbing in and out, running up and down, or being high or low on the jungle gym (Marzoff & DeLoache, 1994; Piaget & Inhelder, 1969).

Group Work and Projects

A small *group* of children can carry out a specific project. Teachers may ask two or three children to go to the school office to find all the machines that are used to communicate, or to be responsible for the plants or pets in the classroom.

Children may form some of these small work groups themselves, selecting one or two friends to join them in creating a mural or doing some other task. Other groups may include children from another class or of differing ages.

To carry out their group tasks, children need to talk and listen to each other. They have to find the words and language to determine the group's goal, negotiate with and convince each other on the ways they will achieve their goal, monitor their progress toward reaching the goal, and solve problems.

This type of informal interaction has been found particularly productive for children whose first language is other than English. Garcia (1996) found that when the classroom was arranged in ways that required children of Latino backgrounds to interact with other children, they asked each other hard questions, challenged each other's responses, and gained higher order linguistic and cognitive skills as a result.

From time to time the entire group of children will meet together. Listening to stories, singing songs, making decisions about their classroom, sharing news, or listening to a visitor involves the entire community of children. These thoughtfully planned group meetings are valuable even for the youngest of children. They give children practice in following a common idea, arguing a point, listening to others' viewpoints, and forming their own opinions. More importantly, however, group experiences build a sense of community (Dewey, 1944). By singing together, listening to stories, poems, and rhymes together, and sharing news and information, children feel a oneness with others that is critical to becoming a member of a democratic society.

Interactions with Teachers and Other Adults

Dewey's idea that children's language learning takes place primarily through the process of sharing experiences includes an active role for the teacher and other adults. Arguing against traditional formal education in which a teacher drills children in letter-sound correspondence or some other language skill, Dewey saw the role of the teacher in language learning as more demanding, calling for more intimate, complex interactions with children, rather than less guidance and involvement (Dewey, 1938).

Today, it is recognized that children do not learn in isolation and that adult interaction in children's learning and development is not only valuable, but necessary for language learning (Bredekamp & Rosegrant, 1995; Dyson, 1993). If children are to learn language through experiences, then teachers and other adults need to carefully structure their interactions with children and each individual child so they are within what Vygotsky (1978) termed the "zone of proximal development." Bredekamp and Rosegrant (1995) describe the zone of proximal development as "teaching on the edge of children's knowledge," so children are challenged to new and higher levels of language and thinking and are able to successfully achieve these.

For example, a teacher may show a child beginning to recognize her name that her name is made of individual letters. "Look," the teacher may say, "your name begins with an *H,* then here is *e, l, e,* and your name ends with *n.*"

BRING MEANING TO THE FORM AND STRUCTURE OF LANGUAGE

For literacy to emerge, children need a set of interdependent skills and processes. The processes of learning vocabulary and forming concepts represent children's understanding of the context in which they are learning language. But other processes are also vital to gaining meaning from the spoken or printed word. Without knowledge of the form and structure of language—printed units of letters and words and letter-sound correspondence, or phoneme awareness—children will fail to learn to use the written word.

Put another way, the child who has a lot of knowledge of the world, who has concepts of hats and oranges and apples, yet who cannot translate a sequence of graphemes into sounds, could not learn to read. On the other hand, a child who can only translate graphemes into sounds and has neither an understanding of the world nor a store of concepts cannot understand what she or he is sounding out and would not be able to bring meaning to the spoken and printed word.

Unlike concepts that are constructed by the child, the form and structure of language—phonemes and graphemes—are social knowledge. Social knowledge is taught or told to children. It cannot be constructed. Children have to be taught that a series of letters is a word, that this word is made of different sounds, and that these sounds can be translated into printed symbols.

While there is some research suggesting that children can learn words, phonemes, and graphemes through rote drill and practice (Byrne & Fielding-Barnsley 1993, 1995), others claim that these are best learned within the context of meaningful experiences (Castle, Riach, & Nicholson, 1994; Stahl, McKenna, & Pagnucco, 1995). Structuring the curriculum around meaningful experiences provides the context through which children can learn the social knowledge of words, their sounds, and printed images.

Social knowledge is intentionally taught to children. But before teachers do so, they ask themselves the following:

- Why is this worthwhile for this group of children or this individual child? For instance, what knowledge of phonemes and graphemes do 3-, 4-, or 5-year-old children need? How would information about these relate to what children already know? How can they use this information?

- What are the prerequisite skills and knowledge a child needs before mastering this particular language skill?

- Why does this child or group need to learn it now? It may be important to learn letter-sound correspondence or sentence structure, but is this something a child needs to know now?

- How efficient is it to teach this to children of this age? There is no trick to teaching young children to do many things—recite the alphabet and name the semantic units; the question is, however, will children learn these things more completely, and efficiently, when they are older?

- Will children experience success and come to think of themselves as learners, who can and will achieve (Bredekamp & Copple, 1997)?

LEARN TO THINK AND REFLECT

Just as language and experiences go together, so thought and language go together. Piaget and Inhelder (1969) argued that language development depends on thinking. Piaget believed children need to have sensorimotor thoughts about objects before they are able to use language. On the other hand, Vygotsky (1986) believed that thought and language develop hand in hand. The child learns to talk about the things she or he experiences. This talking, the new vocabulary mastered, in turn influences the form and content of the child's thinking.

Regardless of which approach you accept, there is no doubt that thinking and language are interrelated. As Dewey (1944) maintained, not all experiences are equally educative. He believed that an experience is not complete until children are able to think and reflect on that experience and communicate it to others (Dewey, 1938).

Children need the time and opportunity to *pull away* and be by themselves so they can think and reflect on what they are doing. At other times, children will be asked to reflect on their experiences by *organizing* their ideas, *presenting* them to others, *applying* their knowledge, and *communicating* it to others.

Being able to *pull away* for a while and think and reflect on an experience is necessary. Thinking involves inner speech. This inner speech is necessary if children are to learn to think logically and to solve problems (Vygotsky, 1986).

For example, young children in group care or educational settings especially need space, time, and freedom to be alone once in a while. One kindergarten class built a large police car of blocks. Over a month or so, they added seats and a steering wheel. One morning their teacher brought in some wires, a battery, and light bulbs. All of the children tried at one time or another during the morning to attach the wires, light bulbs, and battery properly. Sasha sat alone at a table. She did absolutely nothing all morning except stare out the window or watch the children trying to make the lights on the police car work. Near the end of the morning, she left the table, walked to the police car, and with the help of the teacher and some children, showed them how to attach the wires to turn on the lights. When asked why she let Sasha just sit all morning, the teacher replied, "Well, how would you expect children to think if we can't let them be alone to day-dream? Aren't thinking and daydreaming forms of speech and problem solving?"

In addition to being alone and thinking, pulling away can also mean children will listen to tapes or CDs, view videos, or look at and read books all by themselves. But it is perfectly acceptable to foster reflection by allowing and even encouraging children to daydream, sit and observe others, or play by themselves in a center.

Organize

Language permits children to *organize* their experiences and ideas in different ways. One kindergarten group studied rocks. With the teacher's help, they consulted books on rocks to help them group or classify the rocks they found. Plans were made, tried out, and revised as their work progressed. The children categorized the rocks they found, la-beled them, and placed them on a table. The teacher added photographs of the children taken when they found different rocks. Children wrote or dictated stories to explain the photographs and created a title for the display.

In the childcare centers of Reggio Emilia, Italy, children are often asked to organize their ideas by making displays that document their experiences and what they have learned. One group, after extensively researching dinosaurs through books and trips to museums, organized their knowledge by constructing a large dinosaur of boxes and found objects. In another class, children painted a large mural of their trip to a field of poppies. Both displays included printed text describing what the children had done, how they felt about the experience, and the conclusions they reached.

Writing is used when children present their ideas through bar graphs or other types of graphs to organize an experience. A kindergarten class tasted a variety of eatable seeds and voted for their favorite. The teacher next made a graph of their votes. This group then surveyed others in the center, asking them which seeds they favored.

Present

An individual or a small group of children might make a *presentation* to the total group. Older children can make a written plan of their presentation. Children could tell about their experiences, perhaps showing pictures of the different birds they saw feeding at the window feeder. One small group found poems about birds they enjoyed and taught these to the rest of the children. If children do not want to tell about their experience, they could draw about it, write or dictate a story to read to the group, dance, act, move, sing, or show others how they did something or what they learned.

Apply

Children can be asked to *apply* their knowledge. They might use their knowledge of writing to list questions they want to ask a class visitor, or to make a list of the things they want to do during the coming week. They could make a class book, perhaps a dic-tionary of words they've learned, and write a plan for creating a group mural.

Communicate

Dewey believed that an experience is not complete until it has been communicated to another. That is why children are asked to draw, paint, or write about their experiences, *communicating* their ideas to others.

At times, children might be encouraged to communicate something they've imagined, rather than experienced. Imagination is a form of thinking, and children enjoy drawing or painting an imaginary trip to the moon, illustrating an imaginative story, or creating an imaginary ending to a favorite story.

SUMMARY

Literacy skills and knowledge emerge from meaningful experiences. When children are engaged in hands-on, minds-on, age-appropriate, and continuous experiences, they are actively making sense of themselves in their world. Because educative experiences are embedded in children's here-and-now world, they are instrumental in learning literacy skills and knowledge. Interested in what they are doing, children are motivated to learn more, to meet the challenges of new experience, to use and gain knowledge of language, and to become successful learners.

Experiences continue. When children leave school for the day, they should always know there will be something for them to continue doing when they return the next day. The fact that experiences are based on concepts key to a discipline and to the development of literacy skills and knowledge gives them intellectual integrity. And because experiences are connected to children's homes and community, there is a continuous thread of learning in children's lives.

When they use language, work with others, and have the opportunity to think and reflect on their experiences, children are active participants in their classroom community. This participation prepares them to take their places as knowledgeable, literate, and active citizens of a democratic society.

2

Active Children—Active Environments

The physical environment of the classroom can be a powerful tool . . . for literacy learning.

Catherine E. Loughlin, 1987, p. 1

Knowing the power of the physical environment to affect children's literacy learning, teachers carefully, thoughtfully, and deliberately arrange indoor and outdoor spaces in ways that promote children's literacy learning.

Both indoor and outdoor spaces must be arranged so children can

- engage in meaningful firsthand learning that makes the need for language real and necessary

- develop awareness of the purpose and use of print

- use language, talking, listening, writing, and reading in connection with their interactions with their physical world and socially with others

- use language to manage themselves, convince another of their point of view, and control their social, play, and physical environments

- think through an idea, reflecting on their experiences, and clarify their own thinking

- experience success as they gain new language skills and knowledge

To accomplish this, teachers elect to organize the physical environment, both indoors and out-of-doors, through centers of interest. Centers of interest are areas of the room or play yard that are clearly defined with either actual dividers or suggested boundaries. They contain materials and equipment organized to promote specific types of learning. The materials are carefully arranged so children can see the choices available, and make decisions about which materials they will use, and how (Bronson, 1995).

Taking on the appearance of a workshop, these interest centers, or learning areas, permit children to make choices about how and what they will learn. The areas of interest enable individualization of instruction to take place as children themselves select the materials to use, decide how to use them, and determine the purposes for their use.

The idea is for children to be actively engaged in meaningful learning, either alone or with others. As children work in these interest centers, they learn social skills, especially cooperation and sharing, and they run head-on into the ideas, attitudes, and values of others (Lanser & McDonnell, 1991). Actively engaged with each other and learning, children find the need to use both the spoken and written language real and necessary.

A workshop environment is especially necessary for children whose primary language is other than English. In a classroom structured for active learning, non-English speakers learn English from both formal and informal interactions with their English-speaking peers and adults (Cummins, 1989; Wong-Fillmore, 1991). Further, children from Asian, Native American, and Hispanic cultures are believed to learn through cooperative work with others (Gonzalez, 1996).

The environments, both indoors and out-of-doors, are made deliberately *print rich.* Everywhere the environment entices children to use both oral language and written language. Some of the environment print is in the students' first language. For example, posters, charts, lists, and signs can be printed in Spanish and English if the group includes Spanish-speaking children.

Spaces are also arranged so they are *safe, healthy,* and *inclusive* learning places for children. The *aesthetics* of indoor and outdoor spaces are carefully thought through because children, who are beautiful themselves, deserve to live and learn surrounded by beauty.

ARRANGING INDOOR SPACES

Print Awareness

A central goal of early childhood programs is to expose children to print and develop concepts of print (NAEYC & IRA, 1998). In addition to being featured in each indoor and outdoor center, print is highlighted throughout the room.

Dictionaries are available throughout the room. Some of these may be Spanish to English, or other language dictionaries. Children may have their own dictionaries in which they or their teachers write the words they know or need to use in a story. Individual dictionaries of non-English speakers can include words written in the child's first language as well as in English. Special words relating to a class theme or experience appear on a chart or hang from a mobile, and word cards children use are kept in box dictionaries on a windowsill. Again, these words will reflect the languages the children bring to the classroom.

In the music area and around the piano are displays of the notes and words from songs and illustrations of songs from the cultures of the children. The library area contains songbooks illustrating notes and words, and books of songs children know and love can be put together and duplicated to take home. Poems and chants the children know well may appear around the room on the walls or on charts.

Displays of children's work, clearly labeled in both English and the language of the children, may hang in the room as well as in the hallway, bathrooms, and coatroom. These displays offer children the opportunity to see how print is used to document and explain their behaviors and activities.

Put a printed label wherever and whenever one is meaningful or useful. Meaning is the key, however. Children have no use for a sign hanging from the ceiling that says "Housekeeping" or "Art." Rather, signs and labels inform children and adults of

- something new
- something to do
- something to observe
- something to think about
- something you need to know

Asking children to place preprinted labels in their appropriate places is one way of informing children of a label's meaning (Schickedanz, 1999). Other labels can include pictures as well as words. For example, a picture of hands putting paper towels in the wastebasket along with the words "Towels in the Basket" helps communicate the message of the label.

Health and Safety

Indoor and outdoor learning environments must consider each child's health and safety:

- Check equipment for sharp edges, loose pieces that could cause accidents, or small parts that children might swallow or stuff in their ears.

- Disinfect equipment daily by washing with detergent in water, rinsing with clear water, wiping or spraying with a solution of two tablespoons chlorine bleach and one gallon of water, and sun or air drying.

Planning for Inclusion

Depending on the need of the child, the physical environment can be arranged in ways that enable all children to participate actively and fully in all experiences. To permit use of a wheelchair, remove physical barriers, provide wider paths, and arrange work spaces and activity units to offer shelter from intrusion or interference.

You can reduce the amount of visual stimulation in a given area for children who are visually impaired. Teachers have found that they can add textures or raised patterns to the walls to enable visually impaired children to locate themselves in space. Others find that offering small shelving units, with a few materials on each shelf, is helpful.

Hearing-impaired children require more visual stimulation and less auditory distraction. Felt pads on tabletops, carpeted shelves and other work surfaces, and the clear display of all materials and equipment will be helpful (Seefeldt & Barbour, 1998).

Loughlin and Martin (1987) do not believe that teachers need to reduce the amount and variety of learning materials within a classroom to accommodate the needs of children with physical disabilities: "Rather than reducing the amount and variety of learning materials, or simplifying their level to meet children's handicaps, the host teachers removed barriers for children with special needs by increasing the variation of materials, which also expanded learning possibilities for all children" (p. 211).

For linguistically delayed children, those whose first language is other than English, or those who speak in a dialect, the literacy environment becomes even more important. Children and their parents must see their language displayed on signs, labels, directions, bulletin boards, and posters.

Beauty

Aesthetics and beauty must be considered. The childcare centers in Reggio Emilia, Italy, illustrate the wonder and beauty of environments created with aesthetics in mind. Stepping into a childcare center in Reggio, one knows immediately that the environment has been carefully arranged to simplify and order the children's world as well as surround them with beauty (Seefeldt, 1995).

Open rooms, filled with light and air, are simply and elegantly arranged. There is no clutter, but rather a clear, clean conceptualization of an environment specially arranged for active children who learn through active experiences.

Everywhere you look there is something beautiful to wonder over and ponder. Mirrors of all types are found throughout the center. Bits of mirrors and colored glass hang in front of windows to catch a sunbeam and bounce it back to children. Long horizontal mirrors are mounted near the floor so children can watch themselves as they build with blocks or play with others. In other places, square or triangular pieces of mirrors decorate the walls.

Plants and flowers are ever present throughout the center in classrooms, in lunchrooms and sleeping rooms, and in the bathrooms. Prints and posters of real works of art

(Honigman, & Bhavnagri, 1998), not cartoon characters, hang at children's eye level in halls, bathrooms, classrooms, and lunchrooms. Children's artwork is mounted, framed, and displayed, serving not only to stimulate children to thought and permit them to reflect on past experiences, but also to inform others of their work.

This emphasis on aesthetics in Reggio reflects an appreciation of detail and sensitivity to design consistent with the Italian cultural tradition of creative endeavors (New, 1999). Nevertheless, children everywhere, not just in Italy, deserve to live and learn in environments that are aesthetically pleasing and visually appealing (Seefeldt & Barbour, 1998).

ARRANGING CENTERS OF INTEREST INDOORS

Centers of interest, full of print and encouraging children to talk, write, and work together, appear throughout the room. Each has books related to, and useful in, the center. Because centers demand the use of language, whether by 3-, 4- or 5-year-old children, they foster initiative taking, concept formation, and vocabulary development.

Each room will have specific centers of interest.

Art Centers

Children's understanding of writing begins as they scribble, draw, and paint. Through drawing and painting, children demonstrate their awareness of the differences between print and pictures. Drawing and painting activities also develop children's fine eye-hand-muscle coordination, necessary for them to engage in the mechanics of handwriting.

Centers of interest give children something to talk about, think and write about.

Not only do drawing or painting activities help children develop readiness for writing and understanding the printed word, but through creating art, children learn to think symbolically. To create, children must first think of something—an idea, a feeling, an event, or something imaginary. Then they begin the search for symbols to express their thoughts. Finally, they must find ways to control the media in order to translate their ideas onto paper.

Because art is another language for learning, the room features a variety of art centers. Each day children should have a choice of whether to draw, paint, model, cut and paste, or build. Easels, fresh, thick paints, and a variety of brushes are available everyday. At other times, areas of the floor, or a table or two, can also be used for painting. Pencils, or markers, should be on hand as well so children can print their names on their productions.

All types of drawing materials—crayons, marking pens, chalk, even pencils for 5-year-olds—sit on open shelves for children's selection (Dighe, Calomiris, & Van Zutphen, 1998). All kinds of paper and drawing tools are available, including blank "books" consisting of a couple of pieces of paper stapled between construction paper covers.

Sewing is as valuable an activity as drawing and painting in developing children's fine motor skills, visual discrimination, and eye-hand-muscle coordination. Many teachers prepare a junk box containing every type of material imaginable, along with a sewing box equipped with threads, bits of fabric, buttons, and large, blunt needles. Five-year-olds can be taught to knot thread, implement a running stitch, and do other simple stitches.

One group of five-year-olds used the sewing materials to make puppets of characters from a favorite story and put on a puppet show. Another group used the cloth and thread to make stuffed animals representing those in the stories of Chicken Little and the Gingerbread Boy.

A separate area is set apart for clay and modeling materials. Clay, in fist-size clumps, can be stored in any plastic or other kind of covered container. When boards covered with cloth are stored next to the clay, children can take a piece of clay and a board and express their ideas in three-dimensional form anywhere in the room.

Because the visual arts give children a way to organize, reflect, and present their ideas or emotions, choose art materials that enable children to do so. For example, a group of children took a walking field trip to a tall, narrow building near their center. When they returned, they found long strips of paper had been added to the painting and drawing areas.

In another school, children took a walk to see the cherry and crab apple trees blooming in their neighborhood. The teacher then equipped the easels and painting tables with a variety of pink, lavender, and white paint and papers and placed books about apple trees near the easels. The children read poems and stories about fruit trees and consulted factual books about trees and fruit. The paintings that were produced were indeed splendid.

A center for woodworking gives children other opportunities to re-create the themes in stories. With a great deal of supervision and direct teaching in how to use woodworking tools, followed by practice and exploration, children can actually construct a boat, plane, house, or toy using soft wood and real tools. You could read *Building a House* (Barton, 1990), *The Busy Building Book* (Tarsky & Ayliffe, 1998), or *Making Music: 6 Instruments You Can Create* (Oates & Koelsch, 1995) to spur children's building ideas.

A place for children to construct three-dimensional objects should also be included. Children can use any material. In Reggio, found objects—boxes, feathers, shells, sequins, paper, silk and brocade scraps—rest on open shelves in aesthetically pleasing ways, inviting children to make choices about what materials they will use. A group of four-year-olds in the United States re-created the events in the poem "Wynken, Blynken and Nod" with junk materials, using a cardboard box to represent the wooden shoe, bits of net and sequins for the fishing nets, and other kinds of materials for the fish.

Book and Library Centers

The library area is a place where books are arranged along with tables, chairs, or cushions to entice children to stay and read. Display books beautifully and carefully so that they lure children to read.

The library area is more than a shelf of books and a table, however. It is a place located away from other distractions where children will find every type of book—poetry, stories, folktales, picture books, reference books and materials, even sections from the newspaper specifically designed for children, as well as children's newspapers and magazines.

Big Books (many of these are available in children's home languages) can help children become aware of the conventions of print. These may be in the library or placed on a chair near the library area.

Most teachers, however, find that books seem to belong all over the room. In one classroom, the teacher added Mother Goose and other nursery rhyme books in the housekeeping area. Here children used these to read their babies to sleep. When one group of 3-year-olds was able to observe butterflies emerging from their chrysalises, the teacher placed books about butterflies near the butterfly cage, and the children consulted these as they painted and constructed butterflies. In another Head Start center, children observed a construction site and were fascinated with the trucks, cranes, and earthmoving equipment they saw. When they returned to the room, the teacher placed several books about trucks and construction vehicles in an open box next to the blocks. Children consulted these as they created their own building.

All children should find themselves reflected in these books. Books depicting the lives of children with special needs, as well as children of diverse cultural, racial, and ethnic backgrounds, need to be selected (Blaska & Lynch, 1998). Include books, magazines, and other reading materials in the children's first languages. Many children's classics such as Sendak's *Where the Wild Things Are* (1963) and others have been translated into Spanish. Parents and other members of the community are willing to lend books written in children's first languages for them to use at school. Or parents may be willing to translate a book being used in class with their children (Tompkins, 1996).

Catalogs are fun to include. Children can use these as "wish books" or, if you place two or more of the same catalog in the area, play games with them: "I'm looking at a toy. It's red and black, and children ride on it. Can you find it?"

Mounted pictures cut from magazines and chosen because they depict a topic the children are studying are fun for younger children to sort through and carry around with them. Books dictated or written by the children, or photo albums and stories supplied or written by parents or the teacher, are other favorites. Some library areas also include a flannel board with cut-out stories for children to sequence or retell by themselves or with a group of children, puppets, and a puppet stage.

Some books may be organized as a take-home library for the children so their learning experiences can continue when they are at home. A simple checkout sheet in English and the home languages of children can be mounted above the books with two markers attached. The children can place a check by their name with the red marker when they take a book out and a check with the black marker when they return it.

Writing Centers

All good schools for young children have a place for writing. This may be next to the computer center or consist of several places in the room. Here blank books are ready for children's writing, along with all kinds of pens, markers, crayons, and pencils. Rubber letter stamps, models of children's names, index cards, small chalkboards, chalk and damp sponges or cloth for erasing, picture dictionaries, and every type of paper abound. Stationery, envelopes, stamps (from junk mail), and postcards of every type encourage children to write.

Sociodramatic Play Areas

The primary sociodramatic play area is the housekeeping center, where children engage in playing house with others, enacting out the roles they observe in their homes. Social dramatic play is rich in symbolism and believed a powerful tool in developing reading readiness. When children play "as if" a block were a scissors, or "as if" they were the mother, father, or baby, they are holding symbols in their minds. This ability to think about the abstract, about things that are not present, is prerequisite to learning to read.

A stove, a refrigerator, and table and chairs are essential pieces of furniture. Cartons, wooden crates, or even boxes can be used to represent these items. One center did not provide ready-made furniture, but gave children hollow blocks so they could create and re-create their "house" daily.

The housekeeping area, which is highly appealing to all children, is the place where children find a way to link their homes to their school. Some props may reflect their parents' work world—briefcases, cell phones, computer printouts, hard hats, work boots, or other equipment representative of parents' work. Others props, such as dishes, pots and pans, calculators, tools, baby dolls representing all ethnic groups, cribs, baby bottles, full-length and hand mirrors, alarm clocks, microwaves, computers, and clothes, will reflect children's life at home.

Select materials that encourage children to use written as well as spoken language. You can provide notepads, blank cards and notebooks to make laundry or shopping lists, calendars, discarded checkbooks, address books, and pencils, markers, and pens for children to write with as they play house. Carbon paper, decks of cards, and calculators are fun for 5-year-olds. Reading materials found in a typical home also have a place in the housekeeping area. You might include small manageable sections of the daily or Sunday newspaper, current magazines, phone books, and books.

You want to link home and school, so no two housekeeping centers will be exactly alike or equipped with the same materials because each center will contain props representing the cultures of children's homes. In one kindergarten in which there were a number of children from eastern Europe, a group was having a heated discussion in the housekeeping kitchen about how to use a pierogi press, a tool used in eastern Europe to make a dumpling-like food. The teacher saw this as an opportunity to teach children how foods like dumplings are made by families all over the world, but have slightly different ingredients and different names. Through stories and cooking activities, the children explored ravioli, wontons, pierogies, and samosas.

From time to time, other areas for sociodramatic play are appropriate. When children visit their parents who work in offices, or visit the school's office, an area for office play could be established. A table framed with cardboard walls represents an office cubicle. Telephones, receipt books, bookkeeping forms—anything that looks official and has space for writing—along with pencils, erasers, and markers of all kinds are the office supplies. Staplers, pencil sharpeners, typewriters and other office tools, especially rubber stamps with stamp pads, will be truly enjoyed.

Based on children's experiences with their world, other sociodramatic play areas might be arranged. For instance, if children have visited

- a post office, then a post office with envelopes, stamps, machines to weigh objects, and cubbyholes to sort mail would be created. Children can make their own mailboxes so they can write to each other.

- a fast-food restaurant, then a restaurant with aprons, hats, trays, boxes for food, cups and bottles, a cash register, and pretend money would be added.

- a supermarket, then a store, complete with a cash register, money, all types of food containers, cans, boxes, bags to pack, along with old cash register receipts, and other materials, would be set up so children could reenact their visit to the supermarket, taking turns being shoppers, clerks, bakers, or shelf stockers.

Areas for Manipulatives

In the manipulative centers, teachers arrange age-appropriate puzzles, board games, letter- or word-matching games, bingo games, pegs and pegboards, construction sets, small plastic or wooden blocks, letter and parquet tiles, Tinkertoys, Erector sets, and other materials. All these give children needed practice in visual discrimination, which is necessary to distinguish letter shapes and for word recognition. Because many of the materials also require that children observe, sort, order, classify, and predict, they are believed to foster children's ability to form concepts.

A few sets or regular decks of cards and other materials, such as large beads and buttons, nuts and bolts, washers, seashells, and other objects, are nice additions for sorting, counting, and categorizing. Things for children to string—beads, bottle caps with holes in them, and shoestrings—are enjoyable items.

Board games, such as Cherry Tree, Shoots and Ladders, and all types of bingo games, are important. When playing these games, children learn to take turns and follow groups rules, but most of all, to consider the thoughts of others (Vygotsky, 1986).

Science Areas

Rich with printed language, books, and marker pens and paper to record observations, the science area or areas are places where children can actively experiment and explore both the biological and physical sciences. The materials selected for the science centers should engage children in hands-on, minds-on activity that requires both spoken and written language. One teacher arranged a pitcher of water and small cups on a table next to small containers of instant coffee, tea leaves, dirt, sand, beans, sugar, and salt. She gave the children the problem, "Which things will dissolve in water and which ones will not?" A clipboard with a checklist for children to record their findings should be a part of the center.

Other science centers could be equipped with things to weigh, measure, and balance. Magnets, compasses, prisms, magnifying glasses, and different kinds of mirrors and colored cellophane also promote children's active explorations.

Machines to take apart—clocks, pencil sharpeners, instrument-panel boards (all of which have been safety proofed)—along with screwdrivers and wrenches interest children, who are curious about how things work. One group of 5-year-olds worked for days taking apart an alarm clock and recording their actions in detailed drawings.

Living things might be a part of the science area if they are well cared for and are not safety hazards for the children. An ant farm, created from a discarded large food jar, intrigues children, as does a butterfly farm or a worm garden. Children can chart their observations, which are then displayed around the room.

Block Areas

Blocks and spaces in which to build are essential. Ideally, blocks should be stored on open shelves with a place for each type of block. Storing all rectangular blocks on the same shelf, for example, fosters children's ability to classify. Blocks can, however, be stored in wagons or storage bins with casters on the bottom.

A complete set of wooden unit blocks is the best investment a center or program can make. If these are unaffordable, you can create blocks out of paper cartons. Additional props for block play include toy traffic signs; sets of wooden or plastic farm, zoo, or domestic animals; and toy trucks, cars, airplanes, trains, and boats. These extend children's social studies concepts as well as represent their experiences.

Include poster boards, pieces of heavy cardboard, and markers and other writing materials so children can readily make signs and labels for their block buildings. A crate of books related to the children's theme for their buildings is useful. For example, if children have visited an airport and are building their own airport, the crate would contain books about planes and airports. If they have visited a construction site and are creating their own such site, a crate of books about construction would be appropriate.

Music Areas

A quiet part of the room, away from other activities, can be established as the music center—a space in which to listen to, as well as make, music. Here, children listen to a record, operating a CD or record player by themselves. Or they play with whatever musical instruments they desire. A piano, an Autoharp, a drum, a guitar, shakers, and other rhythm instruments can be on hand. Children, assuming responsibilities, can be taught to handle and experiment with real musical instruments without damaging them.

Music books belong in this center. These might be new to the children or copies of the ones used in the classroom. They, as all other printed materials in the classroom, include songs and music in the first language of the children.

Add lined music paper for children to use to create and write their own songs. Some children use the paper to copy songs from a music book, and others just scribble songs, but some will actually use notes and words to create and record their own songs.

Listening Centers

A listening center with tape recorders, record players, CDs, and jacks so more than one child can listen to a story, poem, or song is another important center. Children can record themselves reading as well.

Computer Stations

Several computers can be set up with age-appropriate programs that

- teach some skills more effectively than traditional and less expensive methods and materials.
- have the potential to help children develop higher order thought skills like judging, evaluating, analyzing, or synthesizing information (Wright & Shade, 1994).
- present accurate information.
- do not emphasize war, violence, or discrimination against women or any racial/ethnic group.
- provide for more than one child to work with a program.

Kindergarten and early primary children can use the computer to write e-mail to each other or create their own Web page. One kindergarten class listed the bus routes and rules, special events, and poems and stories they enjoyed in class on their Web page. Their drawings and their own stories were featured.

Quiet Spaces

Children need space to be alone or with one or two others. It may be a corner of the room, with a few pillows on the floor, a small nook in the library area, or a chair and table somewhere away from the other centers. Every room needs a space—wherever it is, or whatever it consists of—where children can be away from the group, and can relax, calm themselves, and think.

ARRANGING OUTDOOR SPACES

Children need the exhilaration, challenge, and freedom inherent in outdoor play. Rough-and-tumble outdoor play gives children the opportunity to develop feelings of confidence, not only in themselves and their bodies, but also in others and their natural environment. Children with physical disabilities find outdoor play of special value. Here they can strengthen large muscles. Depending on their needs, they can walk up and down hills, climb, and exercise small muscles by digging in the sand or playing in water.

Even though outdoor play is basically for large muscle, physical development and exhilarating play, it also fosters children's language, and their ability to take the initiative, and provides for additional learning experiences through increases in two areas:

1. *Opportunities to cooperate with others, constructing large buildings and objects.* Of course children play cooperatively indoors, but being outside somehow fosters more expansive, and often long-term, cooperative efforts. Complex schemes for rearranging equipment, digging gardens, making cities in the sand, or building structures develop and bloom out-of-doors and call for complex language and negotiation. Labels in the garden, on the city built of sand, and on their buildings make the need for written language real.

2. *Space and time for physical play.* Space and a variety of equipment foster boisterous running, jumping, and climbing out-of-doors. Equipment that promotes social interactions, use of language, and cooperative play and is rich with potential for children to form concepts of the physical properties of their world includes the following:

   - Large wooden crates and boxes, boards with cleats, and large hollow blocks. The size of these materials demands that two or more children talk and negotiate in order to use them for building.

   - Cable tables of assorted sizes, tree trunks with sharp branches removed, and sturdy wooden barrels. These give children the opportunity to use large muscles as well as work cooperatively with others.

   - Balance beams. An old log, several logs placed end to end, a board placed on its side, or stepping stones, patio stones, or old tires placed in a series give children several different ways to balance themselves in space.

   - Things to push and pull. Such items give children a sense of control over their environment. Large wooden or cardboard boxes, planks, old tires, even small cable tables can be rolled to new locations, stacked to make a tower, or pushed around the yard.

OTHER OUTDOOR ACTIVITIES

The out-of-doors is really an extension of the stimulating, well-arranged indoor learning environment. The added richness of the natural surroundings and open spaces enhances possibilities for learning experiences. Centers of interest found indoors can be arranged in varying forms out-of-doors.

Water and Sand

Water and sand areas out-of-doors offer new and varied sensory experiences (Stone & Glascott, 1998). Here children can explore the properties of both elements and develop concepts of the surfaces of the world on which they live. Sand, in a sand table, a plastic tub, or an old wading pool, can readily be available. Water must be handy if children are to build with sand, however. Some teachers, objecting to sand indoors, find they can substitute rice, beans, or sawdust for indoor pouring and measuring.

On a hot and sunny day, children can play with water and hoses or run through a sprinkler. They can wash doll clothes and hang them in the sun to dry, or they can make signs, "Wash Your Car," money, and receipts, and hold a car wash. Children line up to wash all the trikes, wagons, and wheel toys they wish. As they play with water, sand, and mud, children use language, not only to control themselves and others, but in fun. They laugh, chant, and sing-song to themselves as they pour, sift, and dig.

Written language is used to record their observations, as well as their chants. Clipboards next to the sand area, equipped with paper and markers, let children record their work and play. Children will use these in many ways. Some simply make check marks on the pages; others will sketch or write about what they did in the sand and with the water.

Sociodramatic Play

Any kind of structure will do to stimulate sociodramatic play. It can be a playhouse, but more likely a wooden platform, a tepee of bamboo stalks, or a couple of boxes arranged with a blanket over them will motivate children to housekeeping play. Add writing materials, large markers, cardboard to write on, and other tools so children can make signs, write lists, and use written language in connection with their play.

Wheel toys placed near the housekeeping center add to the complexity of sociodramatic play. "Parents" can leave for work on bikes or in wagons, deliveries can be made, or firefighters can come to rescue the "house" and the people in it. Receipt books, markers, and crayons permit children to make tickets, money, or needed receipts for their deliveries and travels.

Art

Any art activity can take place outside. From painting with water to painting on large brown paper strips hanging on a playground fence, children enjoy painting out-of-doors.

Children can draw or write on the hard surfaces on the play yard with large chunk chalk dipped in water. Their creations will wash away with the next rain. Or they can use crayons or markers on large paper spread on the yard or tables. Modeling with clay and other materials is fun to do outside, as is building with large boxes, found objects, and other materials.

Science

With nature surrounding them outdoors, children approach science with dynamic curiosity and vivid interest. Experiences with the biological as well as physical sciences are plentiful.

The life cycle of living things can be directly observed and recorded in photographs, drawings, and graphs. Watching birds, insects, and mammals fosters the concept of the variety of life on the earth. Seeds and bulbs can be planted and cared for. A few butterfly nets aid in the study of insects (Rivkin, 1995).

Clipboards, paper, and markers should be a part of the science areas. If live animals are a part of the outdoors, clipboards with sheets to record when, by whom, and how the animal cages were cleaned and the animals fed will be needed. Other clipboards might include spaces for children to draw on or record data in some other way—the birds they saw, how the clouds moved across the sky, or the seeds or leaves they found in the play yard.

Math

Counting, classifying, ordering, and other mathematical concepts become real outdoors. The smooth stones a child gathers, the acorns another collects, the sticks or cups in the sandbox, the number of children waiting to ride a new trike—all these give children something meaningful to count. Children also classify the stones, insects, seeds, and acorns they find, or place them in order from smallest to largest, heaviest to lightest. Garcia (1996) claims that the more linguistically diverse the children, the more important it is to offer children the opportunity for this type of informal learning in which they can apply what they have learned and are learning to real-life situations.

Organized Games

Organized games, or rule-governed games, that begin and end spontaneously, such as *Ring Around the Rosy, Frog in the Middle, Did You Ever See a Lassie?, Punchinello,* and others, help build children's phonological awareness and memory. The values of playing organized games are many. By playing a game together, children gain concepts of

- cooperating, learning to give up some of their individuality for the good of the group.

- sequencing, learning and remembering what to do next.

- structured language. The repetitive language found in organized games introduces children to concepts of grammar.

THE TEACHER'S ROLE

Carefully arranged environments alone do not teach children. They provide the opportunity for children to engage in the use of language with each other, but it takes the guidance of sensitive, knowledgeable, and highly trained teachers to *actualize* the potential of the physical spaces.

Without a concerned, interested, and knowledgeable adult, even the best equipped indoor or outdoor spaces fall short of offering children meaningful language experiences. Based on knowledge of children, of their experiences at home and in the community, it is the adult who

- selects, arranges, and changes the indoor and outdoor centers, making sure the spaces are print rich and remain uncluttered, safe, inviting, and accessible to all children, including those with special needs.

- schedules large blocks of time during the morning and afternoon for free play both indoors and out.

- provides a background of meaningful experiences with people, places, and things so children will have ideas—including the imaginary—feelings, and emotions to express through language and their play.

Most of all, however, it is the teacher who talks with children, interacting with them in ways that clarify, extend, and expand their language knowledge and skills.

- Teachers observe and supervise children as they play. Observations can focus on the total group of children or on individuals. The progress children are making in using language, increasing vocabulary, and incorporating written symbols in their artwork, the other skills they are gaining, and the things they still need to learn can be noted. When needed, teachers step in—giving children words they need to keep the play moving along, or helping them to write a letter or find a word they need to complete their story. Teachers also set limits, clarify rules, and support children in their attempts to learn new concepts, skills, and attitudes.

- Teachers enter into joint activities with children, working collaboratively with them on a problem or task, such as building a block structure, a rabbit hutch, or another specific item.

- Teachers extend children's play by entering into the play scene. A teacher of 3-year-olds subtly encouraged children who were playing shoe store by saying things like, "Where can I pay for my shoes?" and "This would be a good place to display shoes." These suggestions led children to organize and extend their play.

- Teachers use language to promote children's learning, naming things in the children's environment and giving information: "That sign says stop. When we see it, we stop and look both ways before crossing the street."

- Teachers ask a variety of questions that lead children to new learning: "Let's count the acorns; how many do you have?" "What colors are you going to use in your painting?" "Is your suitcase light or heavy?" "Where do I buy my ticket?"

- Teachers offer assistance to help a child solve a problem or achieve the next level of functioning: "Here, I'll hold this piece while you attach this part."

- Teachers plan and help children select activities that are appropriate for individual children's development and background of experiences.

- Teachers set expectations for classroom behaviors that are consistent with children's emerging cognitive and social capabilities (Berk & Winsler, 1995).

- Teachers demonstrate how to do something, supporting children as they try.

- Teachers give specific directions and information.

- Teachers seriously enter into conversations about children's work, focusing on the children, their work, and their ideas. Some teachers seem reluctant to engage children in meaningful conversations. You can talk about content the child is exploring, relationships, and what the child is doing.

- Teachers carefully structure their interactions with children that are within what Vygotsky (1978) termed "the zone of proximal development."

- Teachers ensure that all children are able to take part in centers both indoors and out.

SUMMARY

Active children need indoor and outdoor spaces that are specifically designed to foster language. Planning indoor and outdoor environments begins with making certain the spaces are print rich, healthy, safe, beautiful, and accessible to children with special needs.

Indoor spaces are arranged with centers of interests. Centers organize children's environment, let them see the choices available to them, and give them the means to work and play cooperatively with others. The arrangement of outdoor spaces is equally as important if active children are to learn language through active experiences. Not only can children experience large muscle play and activity outdoors, but just being outside enhances children's sensory experiences and their opportunities to observe their world and enter into cooperative play with others.

As Dewey (1938) suggested, the role of the teacher is more complex and more intimate when children are actively engaged in experiential learning. Teachers schedule large blocks of time for children's indoor and outdoor activities, and actively teach, guide, and interact with children.

3

Building Connections to Home and Community
Extending Active Literacy Experiences

Here is the organic relation of theory and practice; the child not simply doing things, but getting also the idea of what he does; getting from the start some intellectual conception that enters into his practice and enriches it; while every idea finds, directly or indirectly, some application in experience and has some effect upon life. This, I need hardly say, fixes the position of the "book" or reading in education. Harmful as a substitute for experience, it is all-important in interpreting and expanding experience.

John Dewey, 1899

John Dewey believed that the classroom should act as a community, a place where young children learn how to function together to solve shared problems. In so doing, children listen to the opinions of others, express their own ideas, and come to some resolution about classroom rules or an investigation into a topic of interest. All active experiences in the classroom require listening to others, speaking, and using written words to pose questions, resolve conflicts, and reach conclusions.

Thus, children learn language within this social context. Books, both fiction and informational, do not substitute for experience, but inform and expand it. Beyond the school, there are important social contexts for literacy learning such as the family and the community. Added meaning is fostered for young children when there are conscious efforts to build connections between them.

Dewey depicted the school at the center with two arrows representing the free interplay of culture, materials, and ideas between home and school. Similarly, he related the school to the natural environment around the school building, and the life of the community as sources for active literacy experiences.

The work of Piaget (1970) and Vygotsky (1986) confirms the importance of building connections to home and community to build language and concept development, although the two theorists differed about which comes first in cognitive development. According to Piaget, "culture acquiring" children construct knowledge about themselves and others within their culture or social world by interacting with other children and adults in home and school. When extra challenge is needed, the broader world of the neighborhood and community provide children with active experiences to build additional concepts and to foster the development of language to organize and express them.

Vygotsky (1978) saw children learning to think and behave in ways that reflect their community's culture by mastering challenging tasks in collaboration with more knowledgeable teachers or peers. For him, language mediates and directs the construction of knowledge so that active literacy experiences have a primary place not only in the school, but in other arenas beyond the school that foster the use of cultural tools.

The International Reading Association and the National Association for the Education of Young Children believe that achieving high standards of literacy for every child in the United States is a shared responsibility of schools, early childhood programs, families, and communities (Neuman et al., 1999). Mayfield and Ollila (1992) argue that "parents are key players in their children's literacy development although they often do not fully realize their strong personal influence" (p. 255). The family has long been considered the child's first and foremost teacher and possibly the child's primary community for learning (Bredekamp & Copple, 1997; Powell, 1989). The effects of parent involvement before school can range from enhancing the literacy environment of the child to severely stunting it, and the effects of parent involvement continue as the child progresses through school.

The whole community can help expand language and literacy activities for children as children experience things to read and write about, or visit children's libraries and bookstores to learn more about books and storytelling. By integrating literacy into the everyday lives of young children, it becomes meaningful, relevant, and powerful. Learning about reading and writing should occur in the context of meaningful activities spanning all areas of the curriculum. Written language, like oral language, is learned by doing things in the real world (Novick, 2000).

BUILDING CONNECTIONS WITH THE NEIGHBORHOOD AND COMMUNITY

Communities have many specialists who are available as resources for classes and for individual children. Storytellers, puppeteers, children's librarians, and media specialists enrich the literacy environment in the school and classroom. Active children build new concepts, information, and vocabulary through excursions into the broader school environment and the neighborhood and community. Print and language are all around as children explore the larger world.

Children's knowledge grows through field experiences such as a trip to the post office, pizza restaurant, zoo, or children's bookstore. Since literacy is integrated into every subject matter area, the purpose of the trip is not as important as the concepts of reading and writing that children get from it. This learning is maximized when teachers lay the groundwork beforehand. Prior to a field experience, the teacher will want to read the children a relevant book or show them a video. This enables children to construct preliminary ideas about what a place is like and what goes on there. By giving children some vocabulary and information in advance, about the birds to be found in the zoo, for example, teachers heighten their attentiveness during the trip. "We can invite children to predict what they will be seeing and hearing, record their ideas for them or have them do so, and revisit these ideas on return" (Neuman et al., 1999, p. 59).

A Teacher's Plan for Meaningful Experiences in the Neighborhood and Community

Mr. Gordon, a teacher of 4-year-olds, had attended some summer workshops on the teaching of reading and writing and became convinced that it was necessary for him to build connections with the wider community through well-planned excursions. Using his experience from the workshops, and the help of his colleagues, he formulated the following criteria for experiences with integrity and meaning:

- There is a continuity of experience as one builds upon another. Mr. Porter had some difficulty with the policy of his school to take a field trip each week to a different place, and realized that the children were having a series of isolated experiences that were soon forgotten. Instead, building experiences around one theme or concept area would help children construct knowledge in depth and generalize it to other areas.

- Each experience is worth the child's and teacher's time and effort. A trip to the play at the community center had been long and exhausting. Since other school groups were in attendance, the children felt small and crowded. Worse, the community players had not been able to provide any advance information on the production so the children could be informed. Also, the vocabulary was too difficult for most of the children, although the play had been advertised for preschool use. The children whined, fidgeted, and started poking and fighting with one another. When asked later what they remembered about the trip, the children said they were hot, they could not hear, and they had to go to the bathroom.

- Advanced organizers should be provided for the children. Children need opportunities to discuss, read about, and role-play the excursion in advance. Some teachers find that asking children to make a list of what they already know, what they want to see, and what they think they will see on the trip is helpful. After a visit to the birdhouse at the zoo, children can compare their list with the actual experience.

- Children should have time to reflect upon and follow up on experiences with plans and projects that enhance and expand their learning. "It is through their own subsequent activities, such as projects and play, that they explore and assimilate their new learning. Children experiment and share the fragments of information and limited understandings that each has gleaned, fitting them together and making the knowledge their own" (Neuman et al., 1999, p. 68). The visible products of such experimentation, in addition to discussions with groups and individual children, allow teachers to see what the children have understood and what misconceptions they may have.

- A planned experience should either be an outgrowth of children's deep interests or meet a specific need for the children in learning subject matter content.

- Flexibility is essential. While most outside experiences are well planned in advance, teachers can capitalize on incidental learnings, such as when children spot an interesting sign, a menu in the window of a restaurant, or a new book at the library.

In planning for meaningful experiences for children, teachers prepare the children, but they also prepare themselves. The purpose of a trip is to provide children with firsthand experiences, based on their interests, that they would be unable to have in the classroom, in school, or on the immediate grounds. In fact, the first step for the teacher might be to decide if the purpose could be accomplished another way. Do the children need to go to the large auditorium to see the dance performance, or would it be possible to bring one or two dancers to the school to enhance the concepts and language of movement? There are many experiences with reading and writing that can occur in the larger school building as children visit the principal's office for an interview, map and chart the hallways, and list the duties of various school employees after observing their work.

Teachers will want to become familiar with the community and its resources prior to planning any trip. Unforeseen difficulties can be avoided if teachers preview the site and talk with the people at the places they wish to visit. Some sites such as museums and libraries have prepared tours and materials for children; however, these may be too long or complex for many. Teachers may shorten and modify an experience when necessary and create their own materials that will be age appropriate and meet the developmental and cultural characteristics of their group.

Teachers will also want to consider the integrative power of a field trip (Seefeldt, 1997). How will the trip to the children's museum facilitate growth in literacy, mathematics, the use of books, writing, the arts, and social skills? As teachers prepare the children, they will emphasize active experiences in all of these areas. In addition, they will chose children's literature that integrates reading and writing with all areas of the curriculum. Each active experience will involve learning new vocabulary words and investigating the site through informational books and fiction. Children will want to draw pictures, dictate stories, and sing songs about what they have done. They will re-create and reinvent their learnings through dramatic play inside and outside the classroom. Social skills develop as children experience new people and places and acquire behaviors to fit the situation.

Some Basic Guidelines for Meaningful Field Experiences

1. Keep the experience simple for very young children, and increase the complexity as developmentally appropriate. For example, very young children will profit from a short walk to the post office to mail a letter.

SOME SAFETY TIPS FOR FIELD EXPERIENCES

- Obtain parental permission for children to participate in the excursion.
- Check the environment ahead, both inside and out, for any hazards.
- Be sure all teachers and staff members are trained in first aid and CPR.
- Take a first-aid kit with you on the trip.
- Take an up-to-date list of emergency phone numbers for each child.
- Check medical forms for children's allergies (including reactions to wasp and bee stings and foods).
- Always walk on the left, facing traffic.
- Be sure that children understand that wild animals are for observation and not for handling.
- Educate children about poisonous plants and drinking water from streams in the outdoor environment.
- When utilizing transportation, make sure the children know, have practiced, and will follow the rules.
- Consider adult/child ratios. Include no more than three or four children on a field trip for each adult present and fewer if the trip requires complex arrangements.
- Remember that small group excursions may be best for all learners.
- Be sure the field trip site meets guidelines for children who are developmentally different.

---

2. Consider the mode of transportation. Walking is best for most children, yet some field trips necessitate bus or public transportation. When using public transportation, keep the groups very small. In fact, observing the signs and print on the bus or subway is an authentic and active experience.

3. If the classroom is inclusive, consider all aspects of the field experience. Pathways and sites must be barrier free and experiences must be open-ended so that all children profit from the trip. Again, small group excursions may provide a better opportunity for all learners to profit.

4. Prepare children to observe closely and gather data during the trip. Their observations will be used as the basis for many activities in the days and weeks to follow.

5. Welcome parents during any phase of the planning, implementation, or follow-up. Opportunities for parents' participation should accommodate their schedules. Parents need not accompany the children on the trip, but there are many ways they can enhance their children's experiences at home if they are informed of the teachers' plans and activities.

Helping Communities to Help with Children's Literacy

Neighborhoods not only serve as a reservoir of rich language and print experiences for children, but they can band together to further the literacy goals of early childhood programs. For example, Rotary Clubs and other organizations in many cities and towns have forged partnerships with schools. Members make a commitment to read to a child

Book Buddies
Librarian
Foster grandparent program

on a regular basis and establish a caring relationship. Volunteers are trained to work with children of various ages. Similarly, many children's bookstores work with teachers on programs of interest to children and recycle slightly worn books into classrooms. Neuman et al. (1999) suggest that "the whole community can help expand language and literacy activities for young children in child care, Head Start, preschools, and other early childhood programs" (p. 116). Child advocates and teachers can take steps to work with their communities and raise community awareness:

• Approach the local library to reach out to centers and family childcare providers who need their help the most. The children's room of the library is usually a "must" visit for young children. Trained to interact with children at their developmental level, the children's librarian stimulates literacy development with attractive displays of children's literature, reading times, storytelling, and sometimes the use of puppets and other props. The librarian can also help children to identify books that they would like to read in the library or borrow until the next visit. Sometimes, too, a trunk of books can be sent to the school to enhance the classroom library.

   Libraries today are widening their programming to include events for toddlers and their parents, parent workshops on literacy and the criteria for choosing children's books, and media offerings. Yet, they could do more outreach to schools and childcare centers with limited resources for literacy development.

• Ask local organizations and business groups to spearhead efforts to buy books and provide training for teachers and paraprofessionals on literacy. Also encourage them to invite groups of young children to their places of business and to provide them with written and illustrated materials as appropriate.

Volunteers from the community bring added enjoyment to children's language learning.

- Coordinate efforts between public schools, Head Start, and other early childhood programs to promote literacy. Facilitate meetings between staffs. Such efforts would also smooth the transition for children from one program to another.

- Enlist the support of senior citizens groups who want to work with young children and high school/college interns and work-study students. They can serve as volunteers to read to children in early childhood settings as well as provide children with experiences to talk and write about.

THE HOME-SCHOOL CONNECTION

Teachers can utilize the family as a resource for children's learning both in the school and in the home. There is an increased research base on the benefits to the child of family involvement even if the extent of that involvement is small (Grolnich & Slowiaczek, 1994; Marcon, 1992; Stevenson and Baker, 1987).

Teachers and parents may face some challenges in working together. According to Powell (1989), early childhood educators increasingly service families characterized by single-parent households, cultural diversity and ethnic minority status, dual-worker or dual-career lifestyles, economic and time pressures, and geographic mobility. The new demographics of family structure call into question the viability of existing approaches to relations between families and early childhood programs. Yet, frequent contacts cement a genuine respect and tolerance for different family types. Involving parents as active partners in the classroom provides both parent and teacher with firsthand information about the expectations of home and school in the area of literacy development. *also Home Visits*

Classrooms work best and children learn more when parents are involved. Teachers may employ the following multiple approaches:

- Conferences in which teachers provide parents with samples of their children's work and invite them to share their observations about their children's literacy learning and their suggestions for classroom and community experiences based on their children's interests. *Portfolio*

- Use of informal contacts. Busy parents enjoy a brief chat before school, telephone calls, informal notes, and bulletin boards that inform them of plans and programs and invite them to participate in a variety of ways.

- Somewhat more formal contacts through the provision of a Parents' Corner or Family Room where parents may interact around learning materials and other activities of interest to the family. Often these include a lending library with fiction, poetry, informational, and reference books for children, as well as toys and games. These may be rotated as children work on various themes and projects in the classroom and take various excursions into the community. *Parent meeting Our Parents would meet after they drop off their children to walk at the track.*

- Regular newsletters explaining the goals for the week, the rationale for certain literacy activities, and ways for parents to support the lessons at home. Other items to include in newsletters are special events at school, literacy activities that children have enjoyed, special television programs that would spark children's interest in reading and writing, special events for children and families occurring in the community, titles of children's books related to current class themes or projects that parents and children might read together, appropriate magazines for young children, and samples of stories, poems, or riddles that children have written or dictated. Newsletters must be translated for other-language readers, and the teacher should be aware that some families might not read at all, so other means of communication are desirable.

- An open-door policy for parents' observation and participation. If parents are unable to work regularly as paid or unpaid volunteers, they may make or send materials for special projects in the classroom, help on field trips, or come to school when their schedules permit.

- Selection of active literacy experiences for children that can be documented. Children will have products such as drawings with stories, child-made books, and journals to communicate to busy parents what they are doing in school.

A Teacher's Experience in Involving Parents in Their Children's Reading and Writing

Parents support the teaching of reading and writing by the interactions they have with their children at home. When Mr. Gomez, a kindergarten teacher, suggested in his newsletter to parents that they help their children with literacy tasks, he received a flood of calls.

Some parents were afraid that they would do something wrong. Others commented that they did not know a thing about teaching, although they would like to help. Still others were afraid their children would feel too much pressure about reading. Mr. Gomez believed that even though the parents would do an excellent job of working with their children, it was time to get more specific about the things they could do, and to formulate a program for taking advantage of literacy experiences in the home.

First, Mr. Gomez held a meeting to solicit parents' ideas on how to help their children with literacy skills. He was surprised that many parents believed that this would involve sitting at a table and teaching in a formal way. Parents were worried about how well their children could compete with others. Mr. Gomez assured them that pressuring their children to read and write might lead to feelings of inadequacy and rejection for the child. Instead, he asked the parents to think of their home as a natural learning environment. He also pointed out that creating a "print-rich" environment in the home was not costly, but could include recycled paper, magazines, simple writing implements, and borrowed books.

Some parents generated ideas such as reading to children and visiting the library regularly. When parents realized that literacy training was something that was happening in their homes already, they came up with many more ideas. Mr. Gomez utilized some of the guidelines suggested by Neuman et al. (1999), and incorporated the parents' ideas. Then the school generated a handout that was translated into the languages represented by the parents. (See Tear-Out Sheet 1 at the end of this chapter.)

When viewing parents as partners in emerging literacy, early childhood programs have documented a number of successful ideas (Mayfield & Ollila, 1992). The list is not exhaustive, but includes the following:

1. *Bookbag Exchanges.* Children take home books and other reading materials to be read by, with, or to their parents or other family members. Children can either exchange the bags when they wish or on a regular basis. Some bags contain several books on a specific theme such as space or concentrate on one children's author such as Aliki, while others include tapes and books. Parents are encouraged to record comments about their child's responses to the materials.

2. *Visiting Class Mascot.* Ms. Green's child development program had a large stuffed brown bear as a mascot. She sent the bear home with a different child each week accompanied by a journal. The child and parents wrote of the things they did with the bear during the week. It was understood that these experiences could be real or imaginary (Jalongo, 1992).

3. *Take-Home Activities.* Games, kits, and activity packets can focus parents and children on fun activities to foster literacy in the home rather than on flash cards and drills. Plastic bags can be used that include the instructions for completing the project and a list of any materials that would not ordinarily be found in the home. The bags also often contain a sheet on which parents and children can record their feelings about the project. Projects that involve sorting, classifying, matching pictures, or playing simple word bingo are effective and enjoyable for both parents and children.

4. *Calendars and Summer Activities.* Teachers are anxious to have parents continue their literacy activities during holidays and over the summer months. Calendars are useful for recording the active experiences that occur each day, such as making a list for the grocery store, planning the menu for a picnic in the park, or writing postcards to friends from a vacation spot.

5. *Using Television in Literacy Learning.* While for some parents, TV is a convenient baby-sitter and some young children watch excessive amounts of TV, television can be an effective and positive tool in helping children become literacy learners if parents monitor the amount and quality of programs watched. Teachers can send home the TV schedule for the week, highlighting educational programs for children and suggesting questions about the shows that parents may discuss with their children. Parents can also be encouraged to focus their children's attention on specific information and to relate what they are watching to real-life experiences.

6. *Make-and-Take Workshops.* Teachers may arrange a social evening with parents and their children. Refreshments and children's exhibits and activities should be available to attract parents. At the same time, teachers can assist parents in making educational materials such as games, books, and puzzles. Teachers will serve as resource persons to explain the directions for each and the value of the materials for developing literacy.

Parents are also a wonderful resource in the classroom. Even if they cannot volunteer on a regular basis, they can share their talents, occupations, hobbies, customs, and traditions with the class and school community as they are able. Children can be encouraged to prepare for these visits by reading informational books and formulating questions they would like to ask the parents. Similarly, they can document their experience with a parent visitor by writing stories and poems, dramatizing, or creating a bulletin board to present the new concepts they have learned.

SUMMARY

Building and maintaining connections with home and community provide benefits to all participants. Young children need active experiences consistent with their participation in reading and writing. These experiences require careful planning by teachers based upon children's authentic interests. Additionally, one experience should build upon another so that children experience an integrated whole rather than isolated activities that they will not remember.

As the family is recognized as a valuable resource for learning, parents and teachers feel mutually supported and learn to understand and value each other as contributors to the child's progressive acquisition of literacy skills. The home-school connection requires sensitivity on all parts, but is well worth the effort. The teacher is the key to actualizing positive parental involvement in early childhood education programs.

What Parents and Family Members Can Do

Preschool Literacy

- Talk with children, engage them in conversation, give names of things, and show an interest in what they say.

- Read and reread stories with a predictable sequence of pictures or events.

- Encourage children to tell you about their experiences and describe events that are important to them.

- Provide opportunities for children to draw and print, using markers, crayons, and pencils.

- Draw children's attention to print such as signs on streets and in stores.

- Sing songs with simple lyrics.

Literacy in Kindergarten

- Read and reread narrative and informational stories to children. Discuss the stories and ask questions as you read.

- Encourage children's attempts at reading and writing. Do not worry about mistakes or criticize spelling.

- Have children participate in activities that involve reading and writing such as making grocery lists or reading recipes.

- Play games that involve specific directions.

- Have conversations with children at mealtime and whenever you are together.

Expanding to First Grade

- Talk about favorite storybooks.

- Read to children and encourage them to read to you.

- Suggest that children write to friends and relatives.

- Bring something that your child has done in the area of literacy to a parent-teacher conference.

- Encourage children to share what they have learned about their writing and reading.

4

The Form and Structure of Language Learning

. . . the coming together of two essential bodies of knowledge to support literacy development of young children: knowledge of the processes of reading and writing and knowledge of child development and learning . . . is necessary to support literacy development . . .

Susan Neuman, Carol Copple, and Sue Bredekamp, 1999, p. 18

Firsthand experiences in their classrooms, homes, and communities form the foundation for children's emergent literacy. These are like the first rungs on the learning ladder. But unless firsthand experiences lead children to an ever-expanding world of new vocabulary, concepts, and language usage previously unfamiliar, children's literacy skills and knowledge will be limited. Thus, the next step on the learning ladder is the expansion and extension of the language children have gained through their firsthand experiences into a fuller, richer, thicker, and more organized form (Dewey, 1938). This form gradually approximates adults' understanding of the form and structure of language.

Teachers who enable children to turn their direct, firsthand experiences with their world into language learning are the double specialists of whom Piaget (1970) wrote. These are teachers who are engrossed in knowledge of each individual child, what each child already knows, and what each child needs to learn, AND in knowledge of the form and structure of language. Perhaps these teachers are more than double specialists. They are more like triple specialists because they are experts in children, language, and how to bring the two together.

KNOWLEDGE OF CHILDREN

Knowledge of some of the universals of children's growth, development, and learning is necessary. There is wide variation, however, in children's growth, development, and learning. Some variation is due to the differences in the sociocultural context of children's lives; some to the natural variation in patterns of normal growth and development. Even though individual children develop differently, we know from research and theory that children in each age group show certain characteristics.

Three-Year-Olds

- have a vocabulary of about 2,000 to 4,000 words that expands daily
- are learning to use listening skills as a means of learning about the world
- have difficulty taking turns when talking with others
- can pronounce words with difficulty, and often mistake one word for another
- like simple finger plays, poems, songs, and rhymes
- enjoy stories and can tell a story, but often forget the point of the story and will tell about the parts they like or remember
- can understand the concept of drawing and painting using uncontrolled scribbles that are one-directional and less repetitive than the scribbles of a two-year-old

- think in ways that are perceptually bound to one attribute and characteristic—an object can be blue, but not blue and small

- are bound by egocentric thought—they are not "puffed up" with themselves; they simply do not understand that others have ideas and thoughts that may differ from theirs

- play alongside others but not really with them

Four-Year-Olds

- expand their vocabulary from 4,000 to 6,000 words and show more attention to abstract uses

- use verbal commands to claim things

- engage in conversation with others, considering the understanding of the other person

- use language to tease others

- learn new vocabulary when it is related to their own experiences

- can retell a four- or five-step story in sequence

- know scribbles represent something and often name their scribbles; they can differentiate scribbles that look like "writing" from those meant to represent drawings

- understand that print carries a message, identifying labels and signs in their environment

- can identify and name some letters and make letter-sound matches

- begin associative play, playing next to others but beginning to play together

Five-Year-Olds

- are very articulate and can use language to control others, make plans, and solve problems

- have a vocabulary of 5,000 to 8,000 words

- engage in lengthy conversations with others

- show growing speech fluency in expressing ideas

- remember poems, songs, and rhymes

- take turns in conversing and can follow a discussion, listening to another speaker and building on what that speaker has said

- are interested in letters and numbers; some begin to print or copy letters as well as some often-used words

- retell, in sequence, familiar and simple stories

- know familiar letter-sound matches

- count and know colors

- recognize that one can get meaning from the printed word, and match some spoken words to the written

- begin to play cooperatively, planning play and sustaining the play over time

This universal information about children's growth, development, and learning informs teachers about the potentials and vulnerabilities of young children. This understanding tells us that in general, the younger the child, the more wedded the child is to learning through firsthand interactions with the environment and others.

Three-, four-, and five-year-old children, still in the preoperational period of cognitive development, must rely on firsthand experiences in order to learn language. As they grow and mature, however, they become increasingly more reliant on learning through symbols, through pictures, and through spoken and written language.

Developmental Variations

While we know and understand that universally children's growth, development, and language learning proceed in similar ways, there are great variations in these patterns. The uniqueness of each individual determines a great deal of variation in normal growth and development. Children's cultural background or special needs lead to other variations in human growth and development.

Children from diverse cultures may have difficulty understanding the concepts and ideas introduced in an early childhood setting. The greater their firsthand experiences with things in their environment and their interactions with others, the more rapidly they are able to incorporate the new into their existing ideas.

Obviously, children who are learning English as a second language will have a different pattern of language development (Gonzalez, 1996). Research suggests that when children learn English as a second language, they

- first go through a silent period. They observe and listen to others, prior to speaking in English or taking part in pretense writing.

- follow with a tentative use of the new language. They mix English and their first language as they play and work with others or to make their needs known.

- use less complex syntax and grammar, and speak more slowly than English speakers, enunciating each word clearly when they first begin speaking.

- use very short sentences as they begin learning to speak in English. They may say "Go out" to mean "All the children are outside."

- move from present verb/noun construction to past and future conversations (Tompkins, 1996).

Cummins (1989) found that in about two years many second-language learners are as fluent in English as their first language, but it can take some children more than five years to reach fluency. Regardless, it will take much longer for second-language learners to master the more cognitively complex language skills necessary for learning to read and write (Cummins, 1989).

Children with language delays or speech or hearing problems may also deviate from the norm in their language growth and learning. Often children with a language delay will talk very little or speak in short phrases. Those with language deficits seem to benefit from being with others in a classroom environment in which activity, play, and meaningful experiences are fostered.

There are many resources teachers can use to gain a better understanding of children's general growth and development. Authorities in the field of early childhood, such as Gesell, Ilg, and Ames, whose studies were reported in *Infant and Child in the Culture of Today* (1974); Sue Bredekamp and Carol Copple, who wrote *Developmentally Appropriate Practice in Early Childhood Programs* (1997); *A Joint Position Statement by NAEYC and the International Reading Association, Learning to Read and Write: Devel-*

opmentally Appropriate Practices for Young Children (1998); and *NAEYC Position Statement: Responding to Linguistic and Cultural Diversity—Recommendations for Effective Early Childhood Education* (1995), have identified universal patterns of children's growth, development, and learning.

KNOWLEDGE OF THE FORM AND STRUCTURE OF LANGUAGE

Knowledge of children alone is not enough. If teachers are to expand and extend children's literacy learning, taking children further up the learning ladder, they must also have a solid understanding of the form and structure of language.

Just as authorities in the field of early childhood have identified universals of children's growth, development, and learning, so authorities in the field of literacy have identified the skills and knowledge necessary to become a literate member of our society (NAEYC, 1995; NAEYC & IRA, 1998; Whitehurst & Lonigan, 1998). These skills have been classified as those that children must construct for themselves, and those that are social knowledge and are taught. Those two categories include the following specific skills:

Knowledge That Is Constructed

1. *Learning Vocabulary.* Learning vocabulary—being able to name the things in the world, actions taken upon these things, and feelings and emotions and the words to describe them. The first experience in this book, "What's in a Name?" (pp. 55–66), focuses on vocabulary development.

2. *Developing Concepts.* Forming conceptual knowledge of the world—having a store of concepts to bring meaning to the spoken and printed word. The last experience in this book, "Second Language Learners" (pp. 147–158), is devoted to concept learning.

3. *Understanding Story Sequence.* Being able to tell a story in sequence, becoming increasingly interested in stories, and pretending to read and write. Experience 2 in this book, "Read It Again!" (pp. 67–79), focuses on understanding stories and their form.

4. *Using and Making Print.* Understanding that meaning can be gained and communicated through pictures and print and learning to express oneself through both pictures and print. This is the focus of Experience 6 in this book, "The Symbol Makers" (pp. 121–134).

    By inventing their own spelling, children form their own hypotheses for how letters and letter-sounds work. Experience 7, "Writing Throughout the Day" (pp. 135–145), introduces experiences designed to foster children's abilities to express their ideas, feelings, and thoughts through writing by using invented spelling.

Language Skills That Are Intentionally Learned

1. *Learning the Names of Letters.* Based on the development of visual discrimination and memory necessary for grapheme awareness and in learning the names of individual letters. Experience 3 in this book, "Learning the ABCs" (pp. 81–94), illustrates how children can learn the ABCs in meaningful context, without rote drill and practice.

Research shows a variety and balance of methods are necessary for children to learn language skills.

2. *Learning the Sounds of Letters.* Based on the development of phonological discrimination and memory—the ability to detect rhyme and initial consonants necessary for learning the letter-sound correspondence. Experience 4 in this book, "Listening All the Day Long" (pp. 95–107), focuses on learning to listen with discrimination and purpose. Experience 5, "The Sounds and Patterns of Language" (pp. 109–120), presents experiences intentionally designed to foster children's awareness of letter-sound correspondence.

Research suggests there is no one method or way to develop children's awareness of, or knowledge and use of, literacy skills (NAEYC & IRA, 1998; Neuman et al., 1999). Therefore, a variety and balance of methods and strategies are presented in the experiences in this book.

CONSTRUCTED KNOWLEDGE

Developing Vocabulary

Although a number of factors are involved, it seems children best learn vocabulary by encountering a word a number of times in a variety of different, but meaningful contexts (McKeown, Beck, Omanson, & Pople, 1985). Designing the indoor and outdoor learning environments in ways that demand the use of language is a first step. Planning walking trips into the community also seems especially advantageous. Through these trips, children gain an understanding of the subtle meanings of words, extending their knowledge.

Awareness of the parts of speech can also be fostered through experiences in the early childhood classroom and surrounding community. Though it will be years before children are introduced to the terms *nouns, verbs, adjectives, adverbs, pronouns* or *noun markers* or *determiners,* early childhood programs can begin developing awareness of the parts of speech. Children can become aware of the idea that some words name objects, others name behaviors or actions, and still others describe both things and actions.

In addition to increasing children's vocabulary through firsthand experiences, another goal of early childhood programs is to develop children's awareness of the concept of *word.* Children seem amazingly unaware of the idea that the things they say can be segmented into words, syllables, and sentences. They appear to have only vague notions of language terms such as *word, letter, sound,* and *sentence* that they hear teachers using (Downing, 1973; Whitehurst & Lonigan, 1998).

Most children seem to catch on to the idea that language can be segmented into individual words, and that print maps to speech, word for word, with little spaces in between. Still, not all children spontaneously learn the concept of word, and even those who do often misunderstand the concept.

All children, however, can be taught the concept of word through a variety of child-appropriate activities (Adams, 1990). Language experience charts and "big books" are one way to make children aware of words, sentences, and even paragraphs. When children see their dictated words printed on a chart or book, they see that strings of letters stand for individual words, and a string of words is a sentence.

Research shows that there are four stages in children's development of the idea or concept of a word:

Stage 1—Children do not distinguish between words and thoughts.

Stage 2—Children understand that words are used as labels for things.

Stage 3—Children develop the understanding that words carry meanings and stories are built from words.

Stage 4—Children are fluent readers, fully understanding the relationships between letters, words, and sentences.

Developing Concepts

Conceptual knowledge of the world brings meaning to the spoken and printed word. Good teachers have always been concerned about fostering children's concept development (Bruner, 1966). Concepts are the ingredients for thinking. They are like mental filing cabinets in which related facts are connected and organized into an idea.

Children's experiences with their world enable them to develop spontaneous, everyday concepts of story structure, words, and parts of speech. This everyday, personal knowledge, however, does not automatically lead to a deeper understanding of more conventional ways of using language. Rather these concepts act like Velcro, hooking onto whatever new information, facts, and experiences children are given. The richer the new information, the greater the possibility for children to see the relationship of one fact to others, and to form generalizations that bring meaning to abstract language.

Vygotsky (1986) pointed out that at different developmental stages, children learn different things as they independently act on and interpret their environment, but other people also interact with children, affecting the course of their development and learning. He thought children operate at two levels of thought. One is the stage at which they can solve problems and think without the guidance of an adult or a more skilled peer. The second level is the stage at which the child can do the same task with adult help or guidance. He called this the potential developmental level. The distance between the two levels was termed the "zone of proximal development" (Vygotsky, 1986).

Thus, teachers teach. Bredekamp and Rosegrant (1995) ask teachers "not to water down the learning experience even for the youngest child" (p. 22), but rather to build on children's existing knowledge and experience, assessing and supporting learning. This means teachers not only understand children's existing concepts of the form and structure of language, but extend and expand children's knowledge by doing the following:

- Providing children with all kinds of books—poetry, literature, single-concept, picture, and reference books—that pertain to concepts children are studying. These may be openly displayed on a shelf or table, inviting children to extend and expand their ideas of a given concept. Some of the books children can use independently; others you will want to read to the entire group or to an individual child or two.

- Looking at pictures and other print media with children. Videos, photographs, movies, and slides, as well as pictures of places and things in, or not in, their environment can be examined and discussed to extend and expand children's knowledge.

- Showing and telling children how they can do something. Teachers, working collaboratively with children, can demonstrate how to join two pieces of wood, use a tool, or play a game.

- Telling children a fact or piece of information that will enable them to make sense of language. Much of the form and structure of language is social, arbitrary knowledge. Social knowledge is different from abstract knowledge (Piaget & Inhelder, 1969). Social knowledge, such as "The name of this is *chair*," "The sound of this letter is *ae*," or "Your name begins with a *C*," is simply told to children. There is no way for them to construct it for themselves.

- Questioning children. Ask children what a thing is, why it is this way, and how it got this way to spur their thinking in a new or different way.

- Increasing children's vocabulary by asking them to observe and listen to authorities show or tell about their field: A police officer shows children how the siren in her car works; a veterinarian shows how to care for a dog.

- Having children use the computer to learn a new language skill or fact, find information, or communicate with others.

- Using language to extend and expand on children's ideas.

- Introducing another experience. Based on your understanding of children's vocabulary and concepts in a given discipline, add another real-life experience that will expand and extend these.

- Providing multiple opportunities for children to learn from one another. Children should be able to revisit their existing ideas of the subject matter by freely sharing their view of the world with others and arguing their point of view. Only through interactions with others can children critically consider their existing ideas and revise these to form more complex and conventional concepts of their world.

Without a store of concepts, children are limited to understanding their world by dealing with isolated facts and bits of information. By handling objects and observing things in their world, children begin to connect isolated facts and make generalizations. They compare, classify, and sequence objects and things: "All of these are trees." Children relate new information to their existing ideas or concepts of how the world works, fitting it into their schemes, or ideas. Many firsthand experiences and encounters with their world are necessary for children to construct their own knowledge of the world and store it as concepts, rules, or principles (Piaget & Inhelder, 1969).

Understanding Story Sequence

Understanding story sequence plays an important part in learning to read. With an idea of story, children are better able to interpret pictures and print and to read and write stories. Even 2-year-olds, if they've been read to, have a rudimentary sense of story. Stories are discussed, and teachers engage children in dialogues about the stories. Not only are all kinds and types of stories read to children daily, but children are encouraged to tell and write their own stories and discuss these with others, all of which also helps them develop the idea of story.

Applebee (1978) described how children's ideas of story continue to grow and become more conventional. Children first tell stories in simple declarative sentences that are usually unrelated. These are called "heap" stories because the organization of early stories comes from whatever happens to attract the child's attention at the moment. Next children tell stories in sequence. These are simple, without plot, and more like a description of some activities a character has done.

By age 5 or so, children develop primitive narratives, with characters, objects, and events put together around some central idea. Some stories are called "chains" because they consist of a series of cause-effect relationships among events. Focused chain stories have plots, but these do not build on the attributes of characters, and in them the ending doesn't follow logically from the beginning. By 6 years of age or so, most children can tell true stories, with a central theme, and the characters and plot are linked together.

Using and Making Print

Print or grapheme awareness and knowledge of the conventions of print—that one reads from left to right, top to bottom, and front to back—are excellent predictors of children's reading success (NAEYC & IRA, 1998). In today's print-rich environment, most children seem to catch on to the ideas that

- print is different than pictures
- adults use print for a variety of purposes
- there are different types of print. There is print on labels, in cards, on envelopes, and in books.
- print holds information
- anyone can produce print

Still, research shows that not all children enter school aware of print, much less the concepts of letter or word, or how to read one (Adams, 1998). Thus, promoting children's awareness of print, as well as teaching them the conventions of how to print, is the goal of early childhood programs.

Learning to Write Using Invented Spelling

Research suggests that children do not learn to spell by being taught phonetically (Ermi & Wilce, 1987). Rather, phonemic awareness and knowledge of spelling seem to develop gradually and over time in print-rich, literacy environments (Adams, 1998). Teachers support children's early explorations of spelling and writing as children draw, paint, and copy, experimenting and inventing their own spelling as they go along (Bredekamp & Copple, 1997; Raines & Canady, 1990).

This support begins by recognizing how children progress from scribbling to writing. As children play at writing, they scribble, print letter-like shapes, or form cursive-like markings, imitating the adults they see. These early scribbles or writing may or may not be intended to carry a message. Often writing is mixed in with a painting or a drawing, but it usually is the picture that carries the meaning, not the writing.

Support for children's writing and invented spelling continues by giving children the opportunity to scribble, draw, paint, and write throughout the day, inventing their spelling as they go along. Doing so seems to develop children's abilities to reflect on their own ideas of letter names, their sounds, and how to express these in print. Further, trying to spell words, according to Adams (1998) and Schickedanz (1999) is believed one of the best ways for children to learn to segment words into their constituent phonemes.

SOCIAL KNOWLEDGE AND SKILLS

Learning Letter Names

Knowledge of letter names is an excellent predictor of later reading achievement (Adams, 1998; Mason, 1980). Children who learn to recite the names of the letters early seem to have a head start when it comes to learning the sounds of the letters and then learning to read (Adams, 1998; NAEYC & IRA, 1998; Whitehurst & Lonigan, 1998).

Thus, a primary goal of language learning in an early childhood program is to ensure that letter shapes become highly familiar to children. Adams (1998) believes that singing the alphabet song and reciting stories such as *Chicka, Chicka, Boom, Boom* (Martin & Archambault, 1989) and rhymes like Edward Lear's "Nonsense Alphabet" over and over again so children overlearn the names of the letters, not only helps children develop phonological memory, but also gives them a memory peg on which to hang the concepts of letters and their sounds.

Developing Awareness of Letter-Sound Correspondence

With knowledge of letter names children seem better able to connect letters to the sounds they hear (Whitehurst & Lonigan, 1998). Learning letter-sound correspondence, as with most literacy skills, develops gradually and naturally over time.

Learning letter-sound correspondence may begin with learning to listen and discriminate between sounds in general, and to listen critically and with purpose. Then children must be able to discriminate and recall the sounds and patterns of their language.

For instance, when children can make up rhyming words and detect them in stories, chants, and poetry, they are developing beginning linguistic and phoneme awareness. With this ability, children seem to be able to learn to read new words in the same family with relative ease. Once a child knows that *cat* and *hat* share the same ending, it seems easy for them to be able to recognize other words of the same family such as *bat, sat,* and so on.

Reading stories and poems and singing chants and songs that rhyme, over and over again, is a good way of introducing children to the idea of word families. Whatever song, poem, or chant the teacher selects to teach to the children, however, should have value as children's literature. Artificial rhyming stories or songs, like the cat on the mat or the ant can't or can, are soon rejected by children as too predictable, without meaning or beauty (Adams, 1998).

Listening to patterned, predictable texts, while enjoying the feel of reading and language (NAEYC & IRA, 1998), is another way children develop the skill of learning letter-sound correspondence.

Saying letter names and their sounds, pronouncing words clearly, and focusing on initial and end sounds of words familiar to children help foster their awareness of letter-sound correspondence. Remember, though, that the more meaningful the experience with letters and their sounds, the more embedded teaching is within the context of children's lives and the more fruitful the instruction.

EVALUATION

Good teachers continually ask themselves, "What are the children learning?" "Which children need extra help?" and "Which are moving ahead rapidly, learning new language skills and knowledge daily?"

Having a clear picture of what language skills and knowledge you want children to gain is necessary. Each of the experiences in *Active Experiences for Active Children—Literacy Emerges* provides clear goals and objectives for children's learning. These goals and objectives stem from those of the National Academy of Sciences Accomplishments in Reading, the joint statement of the National Association for the Education of Young Children and the International Reading Association, and Marilyn Jager Adam's book *Beginning Reading* (1992). Evaluation then, revolves around analyzing whether or not children have achieved the stated goals and objectives.

In addition, teachers find other ways to evaluate children's learning. They observe children informally as they work and play together, talk with them individually to find out what each child understands and what will challenge each, collect samples of work to include in portfolios, and use checklists to determine how children are progressing.

Teachers use a number of authentic evaluation techniques:

- They observe continually.

  Observing children as they work and play yields a great deal of information about their language development, skills, and knowledge. Some observations are ongoing and informal. Teachers can continually make a note of children using new vocabulary, incorporating print into their paintings and drawings, asking for help in spelling a word, or becoming more interested in reading by pretending to read or write.

  Other observations can be more formal. Teachers may focus on the language of an individual child for a given period of time, recording what the child says and does, the questions he or she asks, and how she or he approaches specific language tasks.

- They interview children.

  Interviewing children is a productive form of evaluation. If you want children to learn letter names, you might interview them and ask them to name plastic letters. If you want to find out which children have learned a poem, ask individual children to recite the poem. Or you could conduct more open-ended interviews, asking children to tell you all the letter names they know or to recite the poems they have learned.

  If your goal is to increase children's use of descriptive language or their concepts of story sequence, then you might show them a picture and ask them to tell a story about the picture, or tell what is happening in the picture. You could prompt children by asking, "What do you see?" "What is happening?" "Tell me more."

- They collect work records and portfolios.

  Collecting samples of children's work and organizing these into a portfolio gives you an idea of children's language learning over time. In the portfolio you might include samples of children's scribbles to demonstrate growth from uncontrolled scribbles to representational drawings, or samples of their printing.

Anecdotal notes—recording how children used new vocabulary or used language to solve a problem or work through a situation—are useful additions to portfolios. Some teachers include a log of books children have read, photos of children giving a puppet show, copies of pages from their journals, tape recordings of children telling or reading a story, and samples of their dictated or written stories and work.

• They use checklists and rating scales.

Checklists, such as those found in *The Whole Language Evaluation Book* (Goodman & Goodman, 1989), can be used to evaluate children's language learning. Teachers observe children and rate them on their ability to draw pictures, pretend to write, use print, read pattern books, and so on.

• They ask children to evaluate themselves.

Finally, children are asked to evaluate their own learning. Even 3-year-olds can be asked to think about the things they enjoyed doing during the day. Four-year-olds, in addition to thinking about the things that went well for them during the day, can also be asked to think of the things they would change. Fours can also begin to think about how they have grown and what they have learned. By 5 years of age, children can pick out their best writing or drawings to include in a portfolio, decide how completely they gained a skill such as recognizing letter names, and rate themselves on how well they accomplished specific tasks like recognizing words or letter sounds. They can also be asked to identify language skills they did not know at the beginning of the year, or when they were younger, and to tell which skills they want to learn next and how they could learn these (Seefeldt & Barbour, 1998).

SUMMARY

Children's firsthand experiences in their here-and-now world are the foundation for an ever-expanding world of learning new vocabulary, concepts, and specific literacy skills. Teachers who bring children and knowledge of the form and structure of language together are those who have knowledge of children, how they grow and learn, and knowledge of the form and structure of language.

Language learning consists of outside-in, and inside-out processes. The outside-in processes include learning vocabulary, understanding story structure and sequence, and learning the conventions of print. Inside-out processes include developing knowledge of letter names, being able to detect rhyme, developing phonological memory, becoming aware of letter-sound correspondence, and beginning to write using invented spelling.

Evaluation of language learning takes a number of authentic forms. Teachers observe children as they work and play, interview them, collect samples of their work, and ask them to reflect on their own language learning. Teachers reflect on themselves and their own work, as well.

PART TWO

Guides to Active Experiences

1

What's in a Name?
Vocabulary Development

─────────────────────── **FOR THE TEACHER** ───────────────────────

◇ **What You'll Need to Know**

"Look," exclaims 3-year-old Claire showing you some scribbles beginning with the letter *C,* "this is my name!" What word holds more meaning to children than their names? Each child has one—and for each their name is one of their most valuable, unique possessions.

Children's names are filled with meaning. Because names have value and meaning to children and their families, they are a perfect springboard from which to teach the form and structure of language. Using children's names, you can introduce nearly every language skill necessary for learning to read.

Then too, since names have cultural meaning, they can be used to make children aware of the values and beliefs of others. In many cultures, names are chosen because they represent a value of the culture, like Imanti, which is Swahili for "faith," or because the name represents long life, happiness, or wealth.

Familiar with their own name and the names of their classmates, children can begin the study of the names of things in their world. Everything has a name. Not only does every object have a name, but so do our feelings and behaviors, and then we use other names or words to describe these.

◇ **Concepts Key to Vocabulary Development**

• Everyone has a name, and each name was chosen for a special reason.

• A name is a word made of letters that also have names and sounds.

• Other things in the world, including feelings and behaviors, can be named and described.

• Some names consist of several syllables; others have only one syllable.

• Names can be spoken, sung, rhymed, and written.

◇ **Goals and Objectives**

Children will be able to say their name and tell something of its meaning, learn and use the names of other children in their class, and become aware that adults have names as well.

Children will recognize their written name, developing interest in learning to write their name.

Children will clap, jump, or beat a drum to the syllables in their name and in the names of their classmates.

Children will learn the names for things in their world, including feelings and behaviors, make books, scrapbooks, or wall charts of them, and recognize these names as words.

◇ **What You'll Need**

All you need is time and knowledge of children's names. Using children's names to teach vocabulary and language skills will take place throughout the school year. Rather than an isolated one-shot occurrence, focusing on children's names can be a daily part of language learning.

Knowledge of the cultural meaning of children's names will be necessary. You will want to respect each individual child's name as their family name. For example, in Asian cultures, the family name is placed first to emphasize a person's roots or heritage (Morrow, 1991). To become familiar with children's names you could

- ask parents how they want their child to be addressed. If a name is difficult for you to say, ask the parents to help you pronounce it, and then practice until you can say all the children's names clearly and correctly.

- read books about children's countries of origin to learn the values and ways of each country.

- seek out resource persons who can inform you of the values a specific culture places on names and the meaning of individual names.

Children's Books and Poems

Alexander, M. (1994). *A you're adorable.* Cambridge, MA: Candlewick Press.

Browne, P. A. (1996). *A gaggle of geese: The collective names of the animal kingdom.* New York: Atheneum.

Gag, W. (1997). *The ABC bunny.* New York: Paper Star.

Martin, B. (1969) *Brown Bear, Brown Bear what do you see?* New York: Holt, Rinehart & Winston.

Merriman, E. (1966). *It doesn't always have to rhyme.* New York: Atheneum.

Milne, A. A. (1924). *When we were very young.* New York: Dutton. (This volume includes the poem "Disobedience.")

Milne, A. A. (1995). *Winnie the Pooh's ABC.* New York: Dutton Books.

Mosel, A., & Lent, B. (1988). *Tikki Tikki Tembo.* New York: Henry Holt & Company.

Most, B. (1995). *Catbirds and dogfish.* New York: Harcourt & Brace.

Pringle, L., & Potter, K. 1997. *Naming the cat.* New York: Walker & Co.

Reiser, L., & Reisser, L. (1996). *Margaret and Margarita—Margarita Y Margaret.* New York: Mulberry Books.

Samson, S. M., & Neel, P. (1994). *Fairy dusters and blazing stars: Exploring wildflowers with children.* New York: Roberts Rinehart Publishers.

Seuss, Dr. (1938). *The 500 hats of Bartholomew Cubbins.* New York: Vanguard.

Williams, S. (1996). *Mommy doesn't know my name.* New York: Houghton Mifflin, Co.

For Your Reference Library

Morrow, R. D. (1991). What's in an Asian name: In particular a Southeast Asian name? *Young Children, 44*(6), 21–25.

Schickedanz, J. A. (1999). *Much more than the abcs: The early stages of reading and writing.* Washington, DC: National Association for the Education of Young Children.

Other Resources

Note cards, wall charts, paper, and drawing supplies will be necessary. You will also need mural paper and paper to make small books.

◇ The Home-School Connection

Let parents know you are interested in learning more about children's names and will be using their names throughout the year to promote vocabulary development and language skills.

You can use the letter on the tear-out sheet at the end of this experience. (p. 66).

◇ Evaluating and Assessing Children's Language Learning

Evaluation of children's language learning through the use of names will be individualized and authentic.

- *Observe* children to note whether they use each other's names as they work and play together. Which children do not call others by name? Record your findings.

- *Interview* children to find out if they recognize their printed name. Ask each child to find his or her name on a list of the names of children in the class. Also ask each one to find and read any names of classmates they recognize. Count the number of names each child recognizes.

  While you are interviewing children, ask them what their name means. Was there some special reason their parents selected their name?

  Ask children to tell you the name of the letter that begins their name and its sound. You might ask older children to name the letters in the middle of their name and the ending letter and its sound as well.

  Have children clap when you say their name, observing if they clap to the syllables. Record how accurate their clapping is.

- Ask children to *perform* for you by naming as many objects as they can in a picture dictionary or in scrapbooks made by the class. Focus on the names of things you have introduced the children to such as clothing, wildflowers, animals, or groups of animals. Accept the child's home language as well as English.

——————————————— FOR THE CHILDREN ———————————————

1. *Children Will Know Their Names*

Children will be able to say their own names, tell something of the meaning of the names, and learn to use the names of their classmates.

- ◆ Begin by teaching children the names of their classmates. Children who know the names of their classmates are those who make friends easily, adjust to school, and experience academic success. Call each child by name, and encourage them to do so as well. When they say things like, "Her won't play with me," respond with the name of the child: "Ask Schwana if you can be the customer."

  - Take a photograph of each child and make a set of cards containing the children's names. To start, meet with each individual child and ask her or him to name all of the children possible in the photographs. Teach them the names of the children they do not know. Five-year-olds can begin to match the photograph with the printed name card.

• Use name songs and games.

Sing or chant

Oh, oh, the bumble bee,
Won't you sing your name for me?

Point to children who respond, either by repeating the song or chanting, "My name is . . ."

• Substitute children's names for those in nursery rhymes. After children know the rhyme "Jack be Nimble," ask them to imagine the most beautiful candlestick in the world. Have them tell what color it is, tell how tall it is, and describe the decorations on it. Then, after they place the imaginary candle on the floor, ask them to pretend to be Jack. First everyone in the class is Jack; then change the name to Mary, Shawn, and Cassidy "be nimble," "be quick," and "jump over the candlestick."

• Learn the old African-American folk song "Get On Board," which was used by slaves to call to one another, naming those who were scheduled to escape through the underground railroad. The song can be chanted or sung:

Get on board little children, get on board little children,
Get on board little children, there's room for many a more.
There is room for (sing a child's name),
*   there is room for . . . , there's room for . . . too.*

Repeat until all children's names have been called.

• The pure silliness of songs and poetry based on names delights children.

Teach children the jingle,

John Jacob Jingleheimer Schmidt, his name is my name too.
Whenever we go out, the people always shout,
John, Jacob Jingleheimer Schmidt

Repeat, using children's names:

Eunook, Eunook Lee, that's my name too.
Whenever we go out, the people always shout,
Eunook, Eunook Lee, that's my name too!

A. A. Milne's poem, "James, James, Morrison, Morrison, Weatherby George Dupree," in *When We Were Very Young* (1924), is also enjoyed by young children. New rhymes based on the poem can be created. Substituting the names of the children, you could make up a poem such as "Rebekkah, Rebekkah, Rebekkah, went down to the store though she was only four."

• Read *Margaret and Margarita—Margarita Y Margaret* (Reiser & Reisser, 1996). In this story two girls, one Spanish speaking the other English, have the same names, but one is named Margaret, the other Margarita. Have children explore their own names and how they are alike and different in Spanish or another language.

• Eve Merriman's poem "Spring Fever," which begins "Al alabis. Alice amasses. Barbara boasts. Frank frets. John jumps," can be enjoyed by children in the early primary grades. After reciting the poem, children can create their own class poem using their own names: "Alice adores. Barbara bathes. Carl cools."

• What is a nickname? Do any of the children have nicknames? Make a list of these. Read *Mommy Doesn't Know My Name* (1996) by Williams and Schachat. A mother calls her daughter her little pumpkin, chickadee, and alligator. What does the mother mean? Do the children's moms have special names for them?

◆ Now ask children to find out the names of the adults closest to them. Give the homework assignment of learning their dads' and moms' names. Make a list of these names. How many children have the same name as one of their parents?

• Do children know that their teachers have first and last names other than that of "teacher"? Tell the children your names, why you were given your first name, and what your last name means.

• What are the names of the other important people in the school? Send children in small groups with an adult volunteer on fact-finding missions. Have different groups interview the school's director or principal, janitor, cook, groundskeeper, and other workers. Make a chart of the people who work in the school using their names and titles. Add candid photographs of those people at work.

• *Tikki Tikki Tembo* (Mosel & Lent, 1988), the best-loved story of how people in China came to give their children short names, is a perfect book to read aloud to introduce young children to the origin of names. After you read it, ask children to make up the longest, the shortest, or the silliest name they want.

• Before naming a classroom pet, read *Naming the Cat* (Pringle & Potter, 1997). In this story, a family searches for the best name for an adopted cat. Have children nominate names for a class pet, perhaps a new guinea pig, fish, or rabbit. Ask each child to select the name she or he likes the best to narrow the list. Then take another vote to select the final name.

2. *Children Will Recognize Written Names*

Children will recognize their written names and develop interest in learning to write their own names.

◆ Children's names can be used to further the understanding of the connection between the spoken and written word. They are spoken in the classroom and then written over their cubbies, on their paintings and other artwork, and on personal objects. In addition, the following activities make use of their names:

• Make as many lists as you can of children's names. Include English as well as Spanish or other language versions of the names so children from diverse cultures can see that their languages are respected. Children are attracted to these lists. They stand around them picking out their own names and the names of their friends. Children in kindergarten and the primary grades may spontaneously name the letters that begin their names, matching these with the same letters in other children's names. Once children are familiar with their first names, add their last names to the lists.

- Begin the year with a list titled "We Are in Room 4." Ask each child to draw a picture of himself or herself for the chart, or place a photo of the child next to each name.

- Make a list of the children when going on a field trip. You could make a list titled "We Are Going to the Fire Station," or "Who's Going to the Apple Orchard?" Other lists of children's names could be titled "Our Valentines," "Santa's List," or "Our Halloween Parade List."

- A bus route list can include the names of the children riding the different buses. One teacher put the bus route list on the Web page for the class for parents to discuss and talk about with their children.

- "When is it my turn?" Some teachers help children by asking them to sign up for their turn on the swing, at the easels, or to ride the new wheel toy (Schickedanz, 1999). Tie a marker to a clipboard and place the board near the contested activity for children to sign up for their turn.

◆ Using heavy index cards, make two sets of name cards. Print each child's name on two cards. Put a rubber band around each set and place these on the library table, in the housekeeping area, or in the manipulative play area. You can simply call attention to the cards, saying something like, "Here are two sets of cards with your names on them. They'll be on the library table for you to play with."

Three- and four-year-olds love to carry these around and just play with them, filling a container with them and spilling them out again. Older children begin playing with the cards in different ways. They will sort them by those they know and don't know, by boys and girls, or by friends or not friends, or simply match the two identical cards.

You can also show them how to play card and other games with the set. Show them how to pass out the cards and hold them in your hand or just put them on the floor faceup. They can pick a card from their partner's stack and match it with one of theirs. Or they can play a made-up form of "Concentration" by placing the cards facedown, lifting one at a time, and trying to remember where the card is that matches the one they've chosen.

3. *Children Will Be Aware of Letters and Syllables in Their Names*

◆ Just as children's names may be the first word they recognize, their names may be the first way they begin to isolate letters and their sounds. Children spontaneously scribble in letter-like ways and say, "There, that's my name." As children draw and paint, the initial and last letters of their first names are often incorporated into their paintings.

When you see children trying to write their names, you can support their efforts by saying the beginning and ending letters in their names and showing them how to write these letters. You can support them by

- observing how they are forming the letters of their name and offer specific advice: "Make a straight line like this one," or "This is the way you print an *a*. Make the circle first; then add a line here."

- making certain children have access to a model of their name. This could be on 3″ × 5″ cards, lists, or any other form. Then provide many ways for the children to make their names. They could assemble their names using plastic letters, print their names with rubber printing stamps, type their names on the computer, or actually print their names using a variety of markers, crayons, paints, or other drawing and writing tools.

- printing children's names at the top of a small chalkboard. They will practice printing their names and erasing them with glee.

- giving children small paint buckets and old or inexpensive paintbrushes and asking them to paint their names with water on the play yard.

◆ Introduce the children to the concept of syllabication by exploring the patterns and rhymes found in their names.

Begin by clapping the rhythm of children's names:

Ste' pha' nie, Ri' car' do, Jim or *Zach' ary*

Children could use rhythm sticks to follow the beat of their names or find ways to step, hop, jump, or slide when you emphasize the syllabication of their names.

4. *Children Will Learn the Names of Things in Their World*

Each child has a name, other people have names, in fact everything has a name! When children begin to name things in their world, not only are they taking a giant step in categorizing and developing concepts of their world, but they are absorbing the idea of a word and increasing their vocabulary.

- Two- and three-year-olds who seem intent on asking "What's dis? Dis?" and "What's dat?" may be driven by the need to begin to organize and understand the world in which they live. Teachers respond to children's queries not only by giving them the names they seek but by initiating the naming of things in the environment. During children's dressing, bathing, and toileting, teachers say, "Where are your toes?" "Put the zipper here," or "Here is your brush."

- Select catalogs that hold appeal to children such as toy, clothing, and outdoor equipment catalogs. Place these in the housekeeping area and the library area, and let children use them as wish books. One class became intrigued with a clothing store catalog. These 5-year-olds then took a trip to the store. After the trip, the children listed the names of the clothing they thought they would like to have and made murals titled "Clothing We Saw at the Clothing Store" and "Clothing We Do Not Wear."

Then the children focused on different kinds of fasteners. They found that some jackets fasten with Velcro, others with hooks and eyes or zippers, and still others with buttons. They examined shoes next and found that their shoes fastened with shoestrings, Velcro, buckles, or had no fasteners at all. Graphs of the types of clothing and shoe fasteners were made.

Next hats caught the children's attention, and they made a list of the names of the different hats in the catalog and those they wear. The teacher read the Dr. Seuss book *The 500 Hundred Hats of Bartholomew Cubbins,* and the children drew pictures of and made the most outrageous, imaginative hats they could think of.

- Do children know the names of the homes they and other people in their neighborhood live in? Take a walking field trip around your school to identify and name the different types of homes. Besides individual houses, you might find trailers, apartment buildings, town houses, duplexes, condos, or other types of homes. When you return to the classroom, make a list of the homes you saw. You could graph the numbers of each kind of home to see which is the most prevalent.

Three- or four-year-olds enjoy making scrapbooks. Staple a number of sheets of paper between construction paper covers labeled "Homes." Cut a bunch of pictures of all kinds of homes out of old magazines. Then young children are better able to cut around a picture of a home (or not) and paste it in their scrapbook.

- A book about the names of groups, *A Gaggle of Geese: The Collective Names of the Animal Kingdom* (1996) by Browne, is good for older children. This book introduces children to the colorful and descriptive nouns used to refer to groups of animals, from a mob of kangaroos to a crash of rhinoceroses. Children can make their own scrapbook of other groups of animals.

- Read *Catbirds and Dogfish* (1995) by Most. Older children will enjoy the fun of the unusual names animals are given such as spider monkey, dogfish, and dragonfly. As you read the book, ask the children why they think these animals were given these names. Imaginary animals are included, so children could follow up by making up creative names for animals they know as well as those they only imagine.

- Children five and older will enjoy *Fairy Dusters and Blazing Stars: Exploring Wildflowers with Children* (1994) by Samson and Neel. Read this book about the fanciful names of wildflowers. Then take a walk to identify the names of the plants and flowers in the children's neighborhood. In one square block in the heart of London, a group of 5-year-olds found several dozen different kinds of plants growing from cracks in the sidewalk, in the gutter, and along the road. This group consulted factual books about plants, and then, drawing pictures of the plants they saw and labeling these with the correct names, they created their own book and called it *Traveler's Joy and Other Flowers*.

  Younger children can make a scrapbook of pictures of wildflowers cut from magazines. They paste these in a blank book called *Flowers*.

- Obtain some expanding file folders and make a set of pictures for children to categorize. You can cut pictures of foods, vehicles, plants, and animals from old magazines and mount them on heavy cardboard. Show children how to sort these by category in the different compartments of the folder. Once they are familiar with the idea of categorizing, provide illustrations of things that could be categorized into several different groups. An example might be animals that could be grouped into pets, farm animals, zoo animals, or jungle animals.

  Initially children categorize the pictures any way they wish. After a while you can show them how to sort a group of pictures into different sections of the folder. You can place a color-coded dot on the things that go together so children can check their sorting themselves.

- Movements and actions have names too. While you focus on nouns, the naming words, you can also foster children's awareness of verbs, another major part of speech. Verbs are the names of actions, behaviors, or a state of existence.

  Make a chart titled "I Can." Have children list the things they can do using action words such as *run, walk,* and *talk.*

- Other words, adjectives and adverbs, describe things and behaviors. It might be fun to start with a chart about a Halloween pumpkin. Begin with the sentence, "The pumpkin is. . ."

  Then ask children to think of words to describe the pumpkin and list these. One 4-year-old's chart looked like this:

  The pumpkin is _____ .

  The pumpkin is orange.

The pumpkin is round.

The pumpkin is hard.

The pumpkin is smooth.

Or take the children outside to blow bubbles in the wind. Give each a straw and a small paper cup half filled with soapy water. Show them how to blow into the cup to make bubbles. After they've enjoyed playing with the bubbles, ask them to think of words to describe what the bubbles did. One class said bubbles float, break, glide, pop, and fly away.

- How many ways can children walk? Can they walk softly, quickly, quietly, fast, slow, up and down?

- Obtain snails or tadpoles for the aquarium or start a worm garden. As they observe these animals, children will find they need new vocabulary to describe their behaviors, actions, and characteristics. Start a word chart using a hanger. Add new words as children request them.

◆ Feelings can be named as well. Encourage children to find words to express themselves.

- When children are angry, ask them why they feel the way they do and give them the words to describe their anger: *frustrated, needing* or *wanting, lonely* or *frightened.*

- When children are happy, introduce them to the words *thrilled, exalted, delighted,* and so on.

◇ Documenting Children's Learning

The entire curriculum might be found in the study of children's names and the names of things in the world. You might chart this learning and hang it in the hall for parents and children to review.

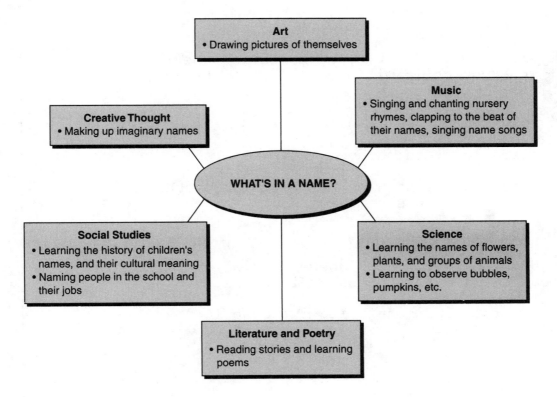

Date

Dear Parents:

This year we will be studying names and their meanings. Your child will be asking you these questions:

• Why did you choose my name?

• What special meaning does it have?

• What is your first name? Why did your mother and father choose this name for you?

• Did you ever have a nickname?

Write us a note with your answers so we can discuss the meaning of different names in class.

Thank you for your continuing interest in your child's learning.

Sincerely,

Read It Again!
Understanding Story Structure

─────────────────────────── **FOR THE TEACHER** ───────────────────────────

◇ **What You'll Need to Know**

When children say, "Read it again," they are letting you know how much reading books aloud means to them. Children fall in love with books and the sounds and patterns of language because you read to them. It's this love of language and books that motivates children to do the hard work necessary to learn to read.

Reading aloud to children is probably the single most important activity in learning to read. Not only are children motivated to learn to read for themselves, but they are also prepared to do so. By listening to stories, poems, and chants, children learn meaning from written and spoken words, and gain new vocabulary and an understanding of the concepts of letter, word, and sentence. They also begin building a foundation of knowledge of story structure, learning that stories have a beginning, a middle, an end, a plot, a setting, a theme, and characters.

Even if reading aloud were not related to learning to read, the early childhood curriculum would be filled with stories. It's through all types of stories—factual stories, folktales, nursery rhymes, and other types of literature—that children come to know who they are, become familiar with other cultures and the diversity in our world, and learn about life itself.

◇ **Concepts Key to Understanding Story Structure**

- Every story has a structure. Narratives consist of a beginning, a middle, and an end; repetitive stories are circular—they begin, end, and begin again.

- Stories consist of characters, plots, and themes.

- Reading aloud to children prepares them for reading by introducing them to the concepts of letter, word, and sentence, and increases their vocabulary.

- Reading aloud to children motivates them to learn to read themselves.

◇ **Goals and Objectives**

Children will develop familiarity with a wide variety of stories, poems, chants, folktales, and other types of literature.

Children will name and request favorite stories and, in some cases, stories or poems by specific authors and illustrators.

Children will know and enjoy stories that celebrate the diversity of cultures in our world.

Children will develop knowledge of story sequence, understanding that narratives have a beginning, a middle, and an end and that some stories are circular and that when they end, they begin again. They will recognize plots, themes, and characters.

Children will increase their vocabulary and develop concepts of letter, word, and sentence.

◇ **What You'll Need**

You'll need a variety of children's books, poems, folktales, and other types of books. Some of these should be "big books."

The Children's Book Council offers free and inexpensive lists of books suitable for children of different ages, cultures, and backgrounds.

Children's Book Council
www.cbcbooks.org/

The American Library Association offers resources for teachers including lists of recommended books and book reviews.

American Library Association
800-545-2433
www.ala.org

Every year the Coretta Scott King Foundation awards books for their multicultural content. Although some of the books are for teenagers or older children, many others will be appropriate for young children.

www.ala.org/srrt/casking/cskaw98.html

Your local librarian will be delighted to help you select books appropriate for your children. The librarian will also help each child receive his or her own library card and demonstrate how to use it.
You will also need

- a long, very special, shiny or velvet "story" ribbon

- construction paper, markers, crayons, and other art supplies

- a puppet stage and materials to make finger puppets

◇ **The Home-School Connection**

You will want to connect families to the curriculum by letting them know which stories, books, poetry, and other literature you are presenting to their children.

- Each month send home a letter listing literature enjoyed by the children. Ask families to read and retell the same stories you read at school. Retelling and rereading seem to strengthen children's knowledge of story structure and increase their vocabulary and readiness skills. (See the letter on Tear-Out Sheet 1 at the end of this chapter.)

- Families have stories, poems, and tales that are representative of their culture or are just loved by their family. Request the names of these stories and other literature so you can keep the home-school connection alive when children are in school.

- Develop a book-lending library. Use a cardboard box or a tabletop. Place a sign-out sheet and a sign-in sheet attached to a clipboard on the table along with books the children have enjoyed that can be shared at home.

◇ **Evaluating and Assessing Children's Literacy Learning**

- Take several times to observe the total group of children. Note how many children elect to look at or "read" a book during center time. Record children's names, the name of the book they chose, and the length of time spent with the book. Repeat this procedure during the semester to determine growth in children's engagement with books over the year.

- Interview children individually asking them to name their favorite story, poem, or chant. Ask them the name of the author as well.

- Conduct a structured interview with each child in your class. Select a book of interest to and familiar to the child. Hand the book to the child and note how she or he holds and handles the book.

- Ask the child to show and/or tell you the title of the book, the author, and, if pertinent, the illustrator.

- Read the book to the child, and note his or her comments, questions, and other actions.

- A day or so later, ask each child to retell the story you read together. Use the checklist on Tear-Out Sheet 3 at the end of this chapter to record children's sense of story. Repeat the book reading and retelling four times during the school year to gain an understanding of each child's growth in understanding story structure.

- Show children a chart of a favorite poem or rhyme. Ask them to frame a letter on the chart and then a word, using their hands. Record their responses. Repeat over time to determine children's developing concepts of letter and word.

- Observe children during free play, noting each time they use vocabulary found in stories and poems.

--------------------- **FOR THE CHILDREN** ---------------------

1. *Children Will Request Stories*

Children will name and request their favorite stories and request stories and poems by their favorite authors and illustrators.

◆ Every day a special time is set aside for storytelling and reading. Every type of literature is valued in the early childhood setting. Picture books, traditional myths, folktales, mysteries, adventures, poetry, chants, realistic fiction, fantasy and humor, and reference and factual books—all are beloved by young children. In general, young children enjoy

> stories about things in their everyday world
>
> predictable stories
>
> stories about themselves
>
> fantasies
>
> rhyming, humorous stories
>
> folktales
>
> stories about feelings, about emotions and handling difficult issues

- Take a trip to your local library. Let the librarian know you are coming so he or she can greet children and show them around the library. Each child can get a library card and select books to take home.

- Reread, retell, and repeat favorite books so children take ahold of them. Follow through by making the books available to children in the library and housekeeping areas, on videotapes, or on tapes or CDs in the listening area.

- Children are naturally attracted to books. Sometimes, though, it's fun to make story time special by setting aside a particular place for it. You might

  have a story rug

  use a long, lovely silken or velvet ribbon and have each child hold on to it as you make a story circle with the "magic cord"

  provide a pillow or story mat for each child

  go outside and read on a mat under the "story tree" on the play yard

  read a story about a boat, sailing, or the ocean while sitting in a boat on the play yard

  call some steps leading to the school or in a quiet place within the school the "story steps" and occasionally read stories while sitting there

- Begin a story by reading the title and naming the author and illustrator. Sometimes you can relate the author to the events of the story. For instance, tell them that the author Robert McCloskey really was Little Sal and Jane's father. Children soon begin to recognize the style of an author or illustrator.

- Discuss the way an author writes: "Beatrix Potter is the author of *The Story of Benjamin Bunny* and *Peter Rabbit*. She wrote about animals that got into trouble but always made it safely back home again. Do you know any other stories about animals getting into trouble?"

- Help children learn to recognize the works of authors and illustrators. Before reading *The Very Busy Spider* (Carle, 1995), you might say, "Look at these illustrations. They remind me of those in *The Grouchy Ladybug*. They are by Eric Carle, the same person who wrote *The Grouchy Ladybug*."

- Make a "Match It" game. Obtain small reproductions of illustrations in children's books, perhaps from advertisements, postcards that illustrate the books, or pictures cut from discarded books by children's favorite authors or illustrators. Mount these on cards and laminate them. The children's task is to match the ones by the same author/illustrator. Color-code the backs so children can check to see if their matches are correct. For instance, the reproductions from books by Sendak have blue dots on the back, those by Fleming, red dots, and so on.

◆ Every once in a while you could begin story time with something special. If you are reading a fantasy story, consult a "magic mirror" to tell you what story to read or tell. Before reading an animal or make-believe story, use a hand puppet or stuffed animal to discuss the story you will read.

- One teacher used a velvet drawstring bag, calling it the "story bag." She would ask a child to reach into the bag and draw out an object relating to the story for the day. One day the bag held a feather and the children said, "We're going to hear the story about little Sal. Listen for the part about the feather." Another day there was a packet of carrot seeds. After reading *The Carrot Seed* (Kraus, 1989), the children went outside and planted a carrot garden.

• While reading and telling a story, be dramatic without being silly. Pausing for effect, whispering ("and fawn came up and kissed her cheek"), or roaring ("Where is my porridge?") helps keep children involved and focused on the story.

◆ Enter into dialogical reading with children. Some magical stories carry children's minds and thoughts to another place or time and can't be discussed after the first reading. One teacher found this out when she read Bill Martin's *Good Morning, Good Night* (1969) to a group of 3-year-olds. When she finished, the children said softly, "Read it again." It wasn't until they had nearly memorized the story that a discussion occurred.

During read-alouds or story telling, both spontaneous and planned dialogical reading will take place. Dialogical reading, with children and reader entering into a dialogue about the story, seems to be highly productive in preparing children for the task of reading.

While reading a story,

encourage children to read along with you, pausing so they can repeat a repetitive phrase: "You can't catch me. I'm the Gingerbread Man." Or ask them to complete a sentence or a paragraph: "I see a redbird looking at _____ ."

make certain children feel free to ask questions, to ask to have a section of the story repeated, or to express themselves as you read.

if children's attention drifts, try using their names instead of the names of the characters: "And then the little red hen said to *Jeremy and Bryan . . .*"

After reading the story ask

What do you think about this story?

Why?

What part was true and which parts were only make-believe?

What would you change and how?

◆ Create a chart of "Our Favorite Stories." When children tell you they have a favorite story, add their name and the story name to the chart. Count which stories are most popular. Or you could make a class booklet of favorite stories with children adding a page about their favorite story. Children can draw, write, or dictate their favorite part of the story or explain why the story is their favorite.

2.   *Children Will Know Stories That Celebrate Cultural Diversity*

All people throughout history have told stories. Introducing children to the folktales, narratives, poems, and songs of others fosters a connectedness between children and people who are far away in space and time.

◆ Read different versions of the same folktale, illustrating to children that people the world over share the same feelings, hopes, dreams, and concerns; for example, the common theme of the physically weak triumphing over a bully, found in the Norwegian folktale *The Three Billy Goats Gruff* (Blair, 1964) and the Mexican tale *Borrequita and the Coyote* (Aardema, 1991), illustrates that regardless of where they live, people share the same feelings.

◆ Reading *The Market Lady and the Mango Tree* (1994) by Pete Watson introduces children to the similarities and differences in shopping in other countries. In this tale, the Market Lady sits under a mango tree. Children could tell, draw, or write about shopping in their country of origin, perhaps creating murals. Then they could compare how shopping is the same and how it differs in diverse cultures.

◆ Read *How Animals Got Their Colors: Animal Myths from Around the World* (1992) by Michael Rosen. This book consists of nine pourquoi stories from around the world. As children listen to the stories, make the point that every culture, across time, has created myths about how the tiger got its stripes, the coyote its yellow eyes, and other animals their distinguishing features.

◆ A storyteller from the local library came to one center and told *A Story, A Story* (Haley, 1971) to the group. Parents then told stories of their own families to their children (see Tear-Out Sheet 2 on p. 78).

3. *Children Will Understand Story Structure*

Children will develop an understanding of story sequence, learning that narratives have a beginning, a middle, and an end and that circular stories do not, and they will recognize plots, themes, and characters.

◆ Before reading a story, ask children to think about how the story begins, what happens next, and how the story ends.

• After reading the story, ask children how the story ended. What did they think of the ending? Were they surprised? Happy? Sad?

• Make story folders. Fold a sheet of 9″ × 18″ construction paper in half, then in thirds. For 4-year-olds, label one third *Beginning,* the next *Middle,* and the last *End.* Cut between the panels. After reading a story with a predictable plot, ask children to draw or write under the labeled panel what happened first in the story, the events in the middle, and finally the conclusion of the story.

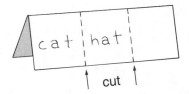

• Act out stories. Have children take on the roles of the major characters. After reading about the Three Billy Goats Gruff, children can reenact the story, taking turns playing the roles of the troll and the goats. Have them discuss how it felt to be the goats and the troll. Do the same with the Three Little Pigs, Goldilocks, and other folktales.

• Retell the story in other ways.

Children could make a mural of the story. Divide large mural paper into three parts, one each for the beginning, middle, and end of the story. In small groups, children can paint their interpretation of the story in sequence.

They could prepare a felt board with cut-out characters to be attached to it. You can use pictures of characters and scenery cut from a discarded, tattered book. Children, individually or with small groups, recreate the story on the felt board.

- A puppet show also demands that children reflect on story sequence. You can create hand or finger puppets in a number of ways and use a cardboard carton as your puppet stage.

◆ Children can tell the story of their lives in sequence as well. Have them make a story folder of their day (see page 73). They could use the three doors to illustrate what they do *Before School, During School,* and *After School.* Or the doors could be used to illustrate what children do

- *Before Going to Bed, In Bed, When I Get Up*

- *Before Halloween Night, Halloween Night, After Halloween Night,* or any other holiday

- *Before a Trip, During a Trip,* and *After a Trip.*

◆ Some best-loved stories are circular, without a beginning, middle, or end. These include the folk song or folktale *There Was an Old Lady Who Swallowed a Fly, Good Morning, Good Night* (Martin, 1969), *If You Give a Mouse a Cookie,* (Bond, 1985), *If You Give a Moose a Muffin* (Bond, 1991), and other repetitive stories children enjoy.

◆ Discuss the plot, theme, and characterization of familiar stories. Often children will begin the discussion themselves with a question or comment.

- You might begin the discussion by asking, Was Tacky really an odd bird? What does the word *odd* mean anyway? What do you think is odd? What would you have done if you were Tacky?

- Talk about the major characters: Which one had the funniest laugh? What did his face look like when he was angry? How would you feel if you were Peter? What would you have done if you had been the peddler?

  What do they think of Curious George? How does being curious get George into trouble? Have they ever been curious and gotten into trouble?

4. *Children Will Increase Vocabulary and Knowledge of Letters, Words, and Sentences*

◆ Book reading, especially of big books, provides opportunities to increase children's vocabulary and familiarity with the concepts of letters, words, and sentences.

- The more times children hear a word new to them, the more likely they are to incorporate that word into their vocabulary. Every story has new words that intrigue and can be repeated to give them meaning.

  In the story of *Peter Rabbit* (Potter, 1997), when Peter's coat became entangled in a net, the birds flew to him and "implored him to exert himself." As one teacher read the story, she noticed the 3-year-olds fidgeting during this section. During the next couple of days when children were having difficulty zipping coats, washing out paintbrushes, or peddling a bike uphill, she would say, "Just like the birds said to Peter Rabbit, I implore you to exert yourself." The next week she heard one of the children telling another whose coat was caught in a trike wheel, "I implore you exert yourself. Pull the coat hard."

- Think of other stories with words new to children. Another teacher found that even though the children loved stories of *Curious George,* they had no idea what the word *curious* meant. She used the word in context over a couple of weeks: "Well, that is curious. What do you think it is?" Or after a child asked a question, "You are very curious, just like George. Let's look it up." Soon children were using the word in their conversations with each other.

- Make a chart of words found in a poem or story that are new to children or that they may want to use in their own writing. For example, after reading the Halloween poem "Brownies Hush," you could make a chart illustrated with an owl and list the words *brownies, owl,* and *quiet* for children to refer to as they write their own Halloween poems.

Brownies Hush

*An owl sat alone on the branch of a tree
and she was as quiet as quiet could be.
Some brownies crept up to the branch of the tree
and they were as quiet as quiet could be.
"Who," said the owl. "Who?"
Up jumped the brownies and away they all flew.*

- Extend 4- and 5-year-old children's vocabulary by asking them to change the words in familiar rhymes. For instance, children love the silliness of Ogden Nash's "I never saw a purple cow. I never hope to see one." What else have they never seen? They could list "I never saw a purple" fish, dog, elephant, dragon, and so on. Or have them change the word *purple.* If you have children in the group who speak a language other than English, they could substitute Spanish, Russian, or Chinese words for the English word *purple,* teaching their classmates another language.

- Do the same thing with extending sentences. Instead of saying "Hickory, Dickory Dock, the mouse ran up the clock," have children describe the mouse. Was it fast, slow, fat, skinny, silly, clumsy?

- From time to time, while reading from big books or charts, use your hands to frame letters, words, and sentences. Say the word, and while framing it with your hands, tell the children, "This word says *misty.* Did you see the mist this morning?" Or you could frame only the letter *m:* "The word *misty* begins with an *m.* Whose name begins with an *m?*" Do the same with sentences. Some 5-year-olds will be ready to frame specific words they know, or could frame an entire sentence.

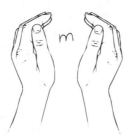

◇ **Documenting Children's Learning**

Clearly, listening to stories enriches children's lives and increases their knowledge of their world. Make a chart of all the learning that stems from reading aloud to children to hang in the school. Illustrate the chart with photos of children reading, copies of book covers, or the names of children's favorite authors and illustrators. Duplicate a smaller version of the chart to send home to parents.

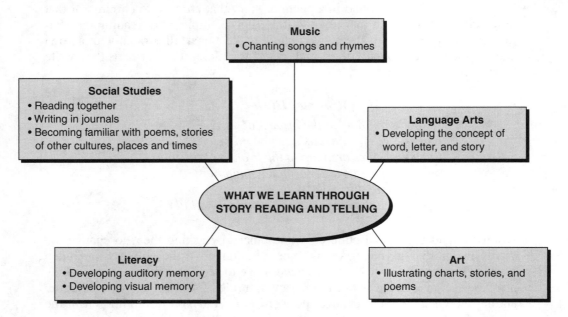

Music
• Chanting songs and rhymes

Social Studies
• Reading together
• Writing in journals
• Becoming familiar with poems, stories of other cultures, places and times

Language Arts
• Developing the concept of word, letter, and story

WHAT WE LEARN THROUGH STORY READING AND TELLING

Literacy
• Developing auditory memory
• Developing visual memory

Art
• Illustrating charts, stories, and poems

Date

Dear Families:

Everyone loves to hear a good story—including your children. Here is a list of books your children have asked us to read again and again:

(list books you have read to children this month)

When you read these books "again and again" to your children, they are learning new vocabulary, the idea of grammar, and the basic structure of stories. This helps them become prepared and motivated to read for themselves.

Sincerely,

Date

Dear Families:

Today a storyteller from the library visited our class and told children the African tale of *A Story, A Story* by Gale E. Haley. We would like you to tell your children your family's stories. These can be favorite stories you heard as a child, or you can tell the story of how you grew up, what you did when you were a child, or what you do now.

Children really enjoy hearing their own story. You might tell them the story of "The Day You Were Born" or "When You Were a Baby." Bring out those old photos, scrapbooks, or videotapes and look at them together as you tell the story of your child's life.

Thank you for helping us keep our curriculum connected to your home.

Sincerely,

Story Structure

Name:

Date:

Checklist   **Notes**

Structure

(Retelling included)

_____ beginning _____ middle _____ end

_____ in sequence

_____ out of sequence

Plot

_____ detailed

_____ unspecific

_____ nonexistent

Characters

_____ described

_____ partially described

_____ not mentioned

Setting

_____ described

_____ partially described

_____ not mentioned

3

Learning the ABCs
Developing Grapheme Awareness

──────── FOR THE TEACHER ────────

◇ What You'll Need to Know

"Listen to me," says 3-year-old Kimberly. "I know my ABCs!" And she proceeds to sing the ABC song. Children as young Kimberly show interest in learning the letters of the alphabet. This may be because they receive a great deal of attention when they say or sing the ABC song—we clap, praise them, and ask them to "sing it again."

Children's interest in learning the ABCs may be a deeper and more complex phenomenon, however. Since the beginning of time, humans everywhere have seemed driven to leave their mark. We find handprints, symbolic drawings on cave walls, and other markings dating back to the very beginnings of human life. These seem to suggest that early on, humans felt the need to record their history, values, and beliefs and to communicate with others through some form of permanent or written language.

Young children, just as their ancient ancestors, seem to realize there is power in written language. Even many 2-year-olds ask to see their names in writing, and by age 3, children want to know the names of letters in their names, asking, "Is this a *B?* My name begins with *B*." And it doesn't take long for children to begin to identify prominent letters in their environment. One 4-year-old waiting in a ticket line at the airport said to her mother, "There's an *A*," and pointed to the gate sign. "And there's a *B* and a *C* too!"

There is another reason for children's interest in letter names. There is overwhelming evidence linking knowledge of letter names to the ability to learn letter-sound correspondence and to become fluent, efficient readers.

This does not mean that all children who learn the letters of the alphabet are successful readers. Quite the opposite! When children are taught to memorize the alphabet in isolation, or through any other methods void of context, they do not experience the same success in learning to read as do children who have learned the alphabet within a meaningful context (Adams, 1998). This seems especially true for children of Hispanic origin, for whom learning letters in isolation seems to decrease literacy learning. Further, teaching the names of letters through sounds without developing the visual identities of letters first also seems to put children at a disadvantage (Adams, 1998).

What this does mean is that reading is based on solid visual knowledge and names of the letters of the alphabet, but that knowing letters is of little value to children unless they are interested in their use (Adams, 1998).

◇ Concepts Key to Learning Letter Names or Grapheme Awareness

- Each letter has a different shape and name.

- Visual discrimination and memory are required in order to learn letter names.

- Knowledge of letter names is a prerequisite to learning letter-sound correspondence and to later reading proficiency.

- Words are comprised of individual letters.

◇ Goals and Objectives

Children will develop visual discrimination by identifying objects and things in their environment that look the same and different.

Children will visually recall shapes, sizes, and objects in their environment, including the shapes of letters.

Children will identify and name specific letters, beginning with the letters in their names.

Children will begin ordering letters through ABC poems and songs and the functional use of letters.

Children will become aware of the fact that words are comprised of individual letters.

◇ **What You'll Need**

Resources

The National Association for the Education of Young Children and the International Reading Association have developed a position statement on early literacy learning that discusses the role of letter-learning. This paper, *A Joint Position Statement by NAEYC and IRA. Learning to Read and Write: Developmentally Appropriate Practices for Young Children* (1998), is available from NAEYC.

Learning to Read and Write (Neuman, Copple, & Bredekamp, 2000) is another resource for teachers. Full of ideas and experiences for children, this book helps teachers plan and implement ways to foster children's grapheme awareness.

A free brochure on phonics and whole language learning is available from

NAEYC
1509 16th St. NW
Washington DC 20036-1426

The International Reading Association offers resources on early language learning that include the role of learning letter names. Their Web site is *www.ira.org*.

Contact the ERIC Web site as well for information on early literacy learning:

www.ERIC.gov

Materials

- An assortment of collage and art materials and small objects
- Sorting trays (see page 85)
- Sets of plastic, wooden, rubber stamp, felt, and cookie cutter letters; letter cards
- Letter board games
- An assortment of alphabet puzzles
- Alphabet books, poems, and other children's books (see book list on page 90)
- Apple pie and cake for a tasting party

◇ **The Home-School Connection**

To involve parents in children's letter learning, you could use the tear-out sheets at the end of this experience.

◇ **Evaluating and Assessing Children's Knowledge of Letter Names**

You can assess children's knowledge of letter names through observations during the day and structured interviews.

- From time to time, observe during center time. Note which children are demonstrating interest in letter names—asking how to spell a word or spontaneous name letters, singing the alphabet song, or using letter names for other purposes.

- Observe children's drawings, paintings, and pretend writing. Note when they include letters in their work and the letters they use.

- Play the "What's Missing?" game on page 85 with individual children to assess their visual discrimination and memory. Record how many objects and changes in objects they can recall.

- At the beginning of the year, select an alphabet book to read with individual children. As you read, ask the child to name the letters before you do so. Record how many letter names each child knows. Repeat the exercise three times during the year and you will have a complete record of each child's knowledge of letter names.

FOR THE CHILDREN

---

1. *Children Will Identify Things That Are the Same or Different*

◆ Learning to read requires the ability to visually discriminate between objects and details. If children's attention is focused on details of things in their environment, they will gain valuable practice in visual discrimination.

- Provide children with collage materials. Each type of material—upholstery scraps, pieces of wallpaper, buttons or beads too large to stuff in any orifice, paper scraps, or nuts and bolts—should be stored in its own individual, clear container. Provide sorting trays made of clear plastic glasses glued to heavy cardboard or discarded muffin tins. Have children sort the materials, classifying those that are alike.
  Children could use the collage materials to create an illustration of

  a new ending for a book they know and love

  what they saw on a field trip

  the beauty of the world around them during the different seasons of the year

- Obtain a bunch of paint chips from the paint or hardware store. Children can play with these by sorting them any way they wish. Show them how they can sort them from lightest to darkest.

- Read *Where's That Insect?* (Brenner & Chardiet, 1993). Children can look very closely to find the 12 insects hiding in the illustrations of this book of insect facts.

◆ Don't forget the role of puzzles in fostering children's visual discrimination. Begin with two- or three-piece puzzles for toddlers, and advance to multipiece puzzles for 4- and 5-year-olds.

- Make your own puzzle, "Match It." Collect postcards or famous works of art. Those that portray children are most appealing. Cut the cards in half, mix them up in a small container, and have children put them together again, matching the bottom halves with the top halves of the cards.

- Show 4- and 5-year-olds how they can make their own puzzles. Have them draw a picture and help them mount it on firm paper or cardboard. Tell them to draw "puzzle lines" on the back and cut the pieces apart. They can mix up the pieces and put them together again.

2. *Children Will Visually Identify Shapes of Objects and Letters*

◆ Before going on a field trip to a fire station, ask children to look at any fire truck they see very carefully so they can remember how many different things it holds. At the fire station, focus their attention on the truck. Back in the classroom, ask the children how many things on the truck they can recall. Compare their list with a Polaroid photo you've taken.

◆ Play "What Is Different?" when you have to wait for a visitor or lunch. Ask a child to select four classmates to stand in a row facing the group. Then ask the other children to close their eyes, and after they do so, change something about the children in the row. You may ask a couple to change places, or one to turn sideways or stand with his or her back toward the group. Or remove a scarf or sweater, add glasses, or have children exchange sweaters. The audience then opens their eyes and tells what is different. Repeat the process, with each child choosing another to take his or her place.

◆ Play "What's Missing?" with individual children or small groups. In this game, children are presented with a tray of varied objects and told to look carefully at the tray. While they hide their eyes, move one of the objects to another place on the tray or remove an object. The children tell what is different.

Play the game a different way to strengthen children's perceptual recall. This time present a tray containing several objects and ask children to look carefully at the objects so they can remember them. Cover the tray and see how many objects the children can recall.

◆ For children to be able to read, they have to be able to see how letters differ. Knowing the letter names does not seem to be necessary for children to discriminate between letters.

Obtain two sets of plastic capital and lowercase letters.

Three-year-olds will simply enjoy playing with these. As they do so,

- give them sorting trays so they can sort by color, shape, or some arbitrary category. Or give them a couple of plastic containers so they can fill them and spill letters from one container into another.

- point out which letters are exactly the same and name them.

- spell their names with the letters, naming each letter in turn

Four-year-olds can

- use a set of laminated cardboard letters and find the plastic letters that are just the same. Name the letters as they do so.

- match the plastic letters from the two sets that are the same.

- find the letters that are the same and different when presented with three or four of the letters.

Five-year-olds will be able to

- spell their name with the plastic letters as you say each letter name.

- find the letter that begins their name and name it.

- use the letters to form other familiar words.

- sort the letters by their characteristics, grouping those that are comprised of straight lines; those of circles and straight lines; and those of horizontal and vertical lines.

◆ Provide children with other alphabet manipulatives:

- alphabet puzzles requiring matching upper- and lower-case letters

- alphabet puzzles in which each individual letter is a puzzle piece so children can experience tactilely the curves and lines of each letter

- computer printouts of letters in different fonts so children can find the letters that are alike

- rubber alphabet stamps

- alphabet blocks

- letters from a Scrabble game

- dial-a-word or turn-a-word games

- cookie cutter letters

- alphabet bingo games

While children use these materials, name the letters and point out their distinctive features: "The *T* is made of two straight lines," "The *C* is like part of a circle," "*S* looks like a snake."

◆ Equip the housekeeping area with letters and words:

- magnetic or felt letters to stick on the refrigerator

- address books placed near the telephone

- rubber stamps with letters or other names

- discarded computer keyboards to play with

- alphabet books and picture dictionaries to read to the "babies"

◆ Extend sociodramatic play to include the grocery store, medical center, restaurant, post office, or airport. Make each place rich with letters and print adding things like menus, appointment books, tickets, receipts, prices, labels, pads of paper and markers, money, advertisements, and so on.

◆ Equip other areas of the room to include letters and print as well. Wooden alphabet letters are for making signs in the block area. Labels and signs can be part of the woodworking area as well as the library area, computer area, listening area, and the science and mathematics areas.

3. *Children Will Identify Specific Letters*

◆ Letter naming and recognition seem to occur naturally when focused around children's names and the letters that begin them.

- Frequently name the letters in children's names. As you write their names on their paintings, name the letters. Point out things in their environment that begin with the same letter their names begin with: "Look, Michele, the *M* on the milk carton is the same as the *M* that begins your name." Show Claire how her name and the word *carrot* begin with the same letter. David begins with the same letter as door, Sabrina as sat, and so on.

- Read ABC books such as Wanda Gag's *The ABC Bunny* (1997), A. A. Milne's (1995) *Winnie the Pooh's ABC,* or another ABC book, and then make your own class ABC book using children's names. It could begin with "A is for Ashok," and continue with "C is for Claire," and so on.

- Group children by the letters that begin their names. How many children are in each group? Make a chart or graph to represent the children whose names begin with the same letters.

- Use the lists you made of children's names and ask individual children to find how many names begin with the same letter as their name, what letter names end with, and how many *a*'s, *c*'s, and so on they can find in the names. When children say a letter name, repeat the name. Make certain that children whose primary language is not English see their names in both their home language and English.

- Make a set of ABC cards. With small groups or individual children, play matching games with these cards and the cards of children's names. Ask children to find the letters that begin or end their name. Find any other names that begin with that sound.

- Make a list of children's names. With each child, decide on the name of a flower, an animal, or anything else that begins with the same letter and print this name next to the child's name.

- Play "Find the Letter" games. While looking at books, magazines, newspapers, and computer printouts or screens, ask children if they see any letters that are in their names. Name the letter and show how it is like the letters that begin or end their names.

◆ Go on an alphabet walk in your school. When you find lettered signs, be sure to read them and point out the individual letters that make up the wording.
    Or you may go on a walk through the school to find

- how many signs say EXIT, and name the letters in the sign

- signs that tell you what to do in an emergency, such as FIRE EXTINGUISHER, FIRE DOOR, and others

- signs that do not have words but communicate through pictures

Venture farther from the school into the neighborhood. The grocery store, fire station, post office, plant nursery, or gas station are replete with signs and letters to read. As a part of their assignment, ask children to look for different letters. You might ask them to find a *P* at the post office, or all the words that begin with *F* at the fire station.

◆ Cut a variety of letters from magazines. Place these on a table with paste, scissors, and blank booklets. Children can choose to paste any letters they like in their book, or only a specific letter, such as the one their own name begins with.

4. *Children Will Order Letters*

Children will begin ordering letters through ABC poems and songs and the functional use of letters.

Three-year-old Kimberly who sang the ABC song and said she knew her ABCs may have been right. Children who can sing the ABC song have an easy time learning to read. Like Kimberly, when children sing the ABC song, they learn not only the names of the letters, but their alphabetic order as well. To make certain all children are as familiar with letter names and their order as Kimberly, fill preschool experiences with ABC poems, songs, and books.

◆ Go to the school's office or visit the local post office and watch the mail being sorted. Have children note the order of the alphabet used on the mailboxes. Back in the classroom, children can create their own post office with small shoe boxes. Help them order these by the beginning initials of their first names. Children can send one another holiday greetings, secret notes, or beautiful drawings as gifts.

◆ Four- and five-year-olds love to be silly, especially when it comes to language. Capitalizing on this, teach children Edward Lear's *Nonsense Alphabet* (1999). It provides children with more silliness than even they thought possible, as well as an introduction to the names and order of letters.

Here are the first three stanzas:

A

A was once an apple pie.
Pidy.
Widy.
Tidy.
Pidy.
Nice insidy.
Apple Pie!

B

B was once a little bear.
Beary.
Wary.
Hary.
Beary.
Taky cary.
Little Bear!

C
C was once a little cake.
Caky.
Baky.
Maky.
Taky caky.
Little Cake!

- Make a felt board of *Nonsense Alphabet*. Find pictures of an apple pie, a bear, and a cake. Mount them on heavy paper and place a piece of Velcro or felt on the back of each. As you chant the poem, place the appropriate picture on a flannel board. Repeat the game, but this time give the pictures to three children and have them place the pictures on the board.

- Have a tasting party. During work time, put a cake and an apple pie on a table. Cut each item into bite-sized pieces and place the pieces in individual cupcake holders. Ask the children to visit the tasting table and vote on whether they like the apple pie or the cake better. Provide clipboards with the labels "A Was Once an Apple Pie," and "C Was Once a Little Cake" and pictures of each item. Under the pictures put boxes for the children to check to indicate their votes. Some may vote for both the pie and cake. At group time, ask the children to stand who liked the pie best, then those who liked the cake the best. The point is not to see if the standing vote and the written vote correspond, but to build a platform for discussing likes and dislikes.

- Read three more stanzas of the *Nonsense Alphabet*.

- Follow the advice of Bill Martin, who said teachers of young children should always "keep a poem in their pocket and a song in their head" (1969), and memorize the first three stanzas of the *Nonsense Alphabet*. With the poem in your head you will be able to introduce it to children in connection with their activities or interests, when it will be most meaningful to them. For example, you might recite or chant the stanzas of the *Nonsense Alphabet* to a child or group of children who

    notice the letters in their names, or in the names of things around them. "Here's a *P*" said Vanessa pointing to the *P* on a the back of a stack of Post-it notes. "It's Paul's name," she explained. "*P*, Paulie, *P*, Paulie."

    chant nonsense rhymes, like Sasha does on the top of the jungle gym. You could distract Sasha from her troublesome chant by responding with the *Nonsense Alphabet*.

- After chanting the poem informally a couple of times, you might introduce it to the total group. The children who have already heard it may chant along with you.

◆ Read other ABC books. *A You're Adorable* (Alexander, 1998) is a charming addition to the usual ABC books. Using the 1940s song "A you're adorable, B you're so beautiful, C you're a cutie full of charm," this ABC book leads to many other activities. One class of 4-year-olds that included a number of Spanish-speaking children translated the book into Spanish. A group of 5-year-olds sang the song to people who worked in their school as a special thank-you.

- Name children's actions and behaviors and make an ABC book titled *What We Do in Kindergarten* (*Childcare*). One kindergarten class started their book with "A is for arriving," followed by "B is for building, C is for climbing, D is for digging," all the way through to "Z is for zipping."

- *ABC of African American Poetry* (Bryan, 1997) is a beautiful, lively, and colorfully illustrated alphabet book. The *Amazon Alphabet* (1996) by Martin Jordan and *Gathering the Sun: An Alphabet in Spanish and English* (1997) by A. Ada are two additional ABC books that introduce children to diverse cultures.
  Some other classic ABC books are

  Carle, E. (1974). *All about Arthur.* New York: Franklin Watts.

  Eichenberg, F. (1952). *Ape in a cape.* New York: Holt.

  Feelings, M., & Feelings, T. (1974). *Jambo means hello! Swahili alphabet book.* New York: Dial Press.

  Greenaway, K. (1886). *A apple pie.* New York: Frederick Warne & Co.

  Hoban, T. (1982). *A. B. See!* Chicago: Greenwillow Press.

  Potter, B. (1987). *Peter rabbit's abc.* New York: Frederick Warne & Co.

  Sendak, M. (1962). *Alligators all around: An alphabet storybook.* New York: Harper & Row.

  Tallon, R. (1969). *An abc in English and Spanish.* New York: The Lion Press.

  Tudor, T. (1954). *A is for Annabelle.* New York: Rand McNally.

- Make your own alphabet books.

◆ Five-year-olds may be able to start alphabetizing things in their environment. You might give them a set of name cards and show them how to begin to alphabetize these. Or you could have them order their favorite colors, the flowers that grow around the school, their favorite flavors of ice cream, or favorite authors by initial letters.

◆ Continue awareness of letter names and their order by using

- alphabet wall charts

- word banks

- picture, box, and wall dictionaries

5. ***Children Will Realize That Words Consist of Individual Letters***

◆ As you read big books, make or consult charts of children's names, and look at signs in the school, frame individual letters with your hands and name the letters.

- You could frame the *C* in Claire's name and ask her to put her hands around other *C*'s on the chart.

- After a big book has become very familiar to children, you could, while reading it again, frame a salient letter with your hands and say its name. Perhaps you could do so with the letter *t* in Fleming's *In the Tall, Tall Grass* (1991). Have children take turns finding, framing, and naming other *t*'s in the book. Do the same with letters in other books.

◇ Documenting Children's Learning

Take photos of children playing with manipulative ABC puzzles, finding letters in their names or on signs, or printing letters. Make a chart for the school titled "Learning the Alphabet." Include a sentence or two from the opening of this chapter to describe how children learn letter names through everyday experiences.

A web documents the integrated nature of learning letter names.

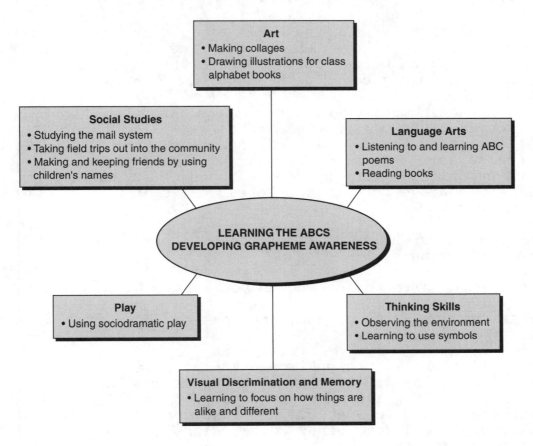

Date

Dear Parents:

Research shows that knowing the names of letters is an important skill. Children who can say the names of some letters will be better able to learn their sounds and to become successful readers.

We will be teaching children letter names throughout the curriculum. This does not mean that we will drill children in letter names. Quite the opposite! The research also shows that children taught through drill and practice do not experience the same success as children who have been taught letter names in meaningful ways.

You can help children learn letter names at home by doing the following:

• Name the letters in their name as you write it.

• Let them see you writing, and name some of the letters you are writing.

• Point out letters in the environment that have meaning for children: "Look at that huge *M* outside of McDonalds." Or while pumping gas say, "Look, Suki, there's an *S* in Sunoco, just like the *S* that begins your name." Read other logos, signs in the environment, street signs, and labels in the grocery store.

• Use alphabet magnet letters to hold notes to your refrigerator. As children play with these, name the letters.

Let us know other ways you and your children informally find letters in your child's world.

Sincerely,

Date

Dear Families:

Today we introduced the children to the poem
"Nonsense Alphabet" by Edward Lear. We've attached a
copy of it so you can enjoy it with your children.

We taught the children the "Nonsense Alphabet" not
just because it is fun and appeals to them, but
because reading alphabet books and poems is one way
children learn the names of the letters and their
order. We have a number of alphabet books in our
book-lending library that you might want to read to
your children. You'll find reading the books we've
selected, such as Martin and Archambault's *Chicka,
Chicka, Boom, Boom,* is a truly enjoyable experience
for you and your children.

Sincerely,

Date

Dear Families:

It is no secret! Children learn through play! And playing with letters helps children become familiar with letter shapes and letter names. We have a number of alphabet games, puzzles, and cards in our lending library for you to use at home with your children.

If you have other letter games that you would like to share with the children, we'd be delighted to have you lend them to us for a while.

Sincerely,

4

Listening All the Day Long
Learning to Listen with Discrimination

―――――――――――――― **FOR THE TEACHER** ――――――――――――――

◇ **What You'll Need to Know**

Children are natural listeners. Throughout the day they are surrounded with sounds. Morning sounds greet them when they wake. As the day progresses, they delight in the sounds of crickets chirping and music and song, and when the day is done, they fall asleep to the soothing sound of a parent's voice singing a beloved lullaby.

Listening throughout the day, children spontaneously identify sounds. They easily recognize and discriminate between the sounds of machines, people, and animals. They readily listen to and memorize the chants of familiar songs and advertisements.

While children's ability to listen to everyday sounds seems to comes naturally and easily, their ability to listen with discrimination, with purpose, and critically seems less natural and far from easy. But because the ability to do so brings joy and pleasure and is necessary for children to become fluent and efficient readers, the development of these skills during the preschool years is critical.

◇ **Concepts Key to Listening Skills**

- Listening skills are incremental. They begin with passive listening, develop during attentive listening, and finally become the ability to listen critically and with discrimination.

- Listening *passively*, children hear sounds but do not discriminate between them or identify specific sounds. Nor do they actively follow the train of a discussion. They may appear to do so but are probably thinking about what they want to say next rather than focusing on the message of the speaker.

- *Attentive* listening is the second developmental level. Children listen actively, attending to what they hear with purpose and to gain meaning and understanding.

- Finally, children listen *critically.* Critical listening demands genuine mental and emotional participation, and enables children to respond to humor, make judgments about what they hear, and react emotionally.

◇ **Goals and Objectives**

Children will develop and refine listening skills while in the early childhood setting.

Children will learn to attend to and discriminate between sounds in their environment.

Children will listen actively with purpose and for meaning.

Children will listen critically, responding with emotion and humor and making critical judgments about what they hear.

◇ **What You'll Need**

- Sound-making objects such as empty pill bottles filled with different hard objects, metal pie pans, and other items

- A variety of rhythm instruments

- CDs, records, or tape recordings of music and sound stories

- A collection of books, poems, and songs including *Peter and the Wolf* by Sergei Prokofiev, the music of John Philip Sousa, and Camille Saint-Saëns' *Carnival of the Animals*

Ginny M. Kruse and Kathleen T. Horning have compiled a list of thirty multicultural books that introduce children to the diversity of cultures in our world through outstanding literature and poetry. You can find this list at

www.soemadison.wisc.edu/ccbc/25mult.htm

◇ The Home-School Connection

The letters on the tear-out sheets at the end of this chapter can be sent to parents so they can continue to foster children's listening skills at home.

◇ Evaluating and Assessing Children's Listening Skills and Knowledge

Document children's ability to discriminate between sounds in their environment:

- Observe their responses to sounds on a sound hunt. How many sounds does each child hear and recognize? Observe at the beginning, middle, and end of the school year to document children's development of listening skills.

- Conduct a structured interview with each child. Place a number of rhythm instruments on a table. Ask the child to pick out the instrument that makes a scraping sound, ringing sounds, or loud sounds; then ask the child to produce long, short, and smooth sounds using the instruments.

Determine children's progress in listening for purpose:

- Play "Simon Says" with the group. Observe which children consistently listen to Simon instead of doing what Simon does, and which do not listen well. Conduct observations throughout the year to determine children's progress in listening for purpose.

- Conduct interviews with individual children after someone has spoken to the group. For instance, you might ask individual children to recall what the firefighter told them, or the directions they were given to get to the school's office. Note how complete, accurate, and detailed children's responses are.

Evaluate children's ability to respond with emotion and to make critical judgements about what they hear:

- Read *Amelia Bedelia* (Parish, 1992) or another humorous book to individual children. Ask them to tell you what they thought was funny and why.

- Observe children as you read to them. Note and record their emotions. How often do they smile, giggle, look sad, or seem to take pleasure from what they hear?

─────────────── FOR THE CHILDREN ───────────────

1. *Children Will Discriminate Between Sounds in Their Environment*

Children are experienced listeners. Building on prior listening experiences, teachers can develop children's attentive listening skills.

◆ Begin with sound discrimination and identification experiences.

• Follow the reading of *Polar Bear, Polar Bear What do You Hear?* (Martin, 1991) by asking children what they hear in their classroom. Make a list of the sounds they hear. Then go on a sound hunt in the school, on the play yard, or through the surrounding neighborhood. As you walk, ask children, "What sounds do you hear in the hallway? In the cafeteria? In the gym? What do the swings sound like?"

Back in the classroom children could make their own books of what they heard. Use their names such as "Sasha, Sasha, What do Your Hear?" instead of *Polar Bear, Polar Bear.* In the books children draw, write, or dictate the source of the sounds they heard on their walk, or in their room, or center, school, cafeteria, or office.

• Read *One Afternoon* (1994) by Ymi Heo, the story of young Minho and his mother going for an afternoon outing. As they run their errands, they discover that every place has a special sound. Take a walk around the school's neighborhood to hunt for sounds. The children may not hear a Laundromat or an elevated train, but every neighborhood has its unique sounds.

• You might ask children to listen to sounds that are near to them and those that are far away. If a siren on a moving vehicle is heard in the distance, ask children to follow the sound as it comes closer to them. Ask how the sound changed as its source came nearer to them. Do the same with the sound of children's feet running on the play yard, planes flying overhead, or birds chirping.

• Begin to focus on differences in specific sounds. For example, most engines make some sort of noise. Ask children to listen to the sounds of the engines of large trucks, cars, trains, buses, jets, and other vehicles. How would they describe the differences in the sounds of these engines?

• Do all birds sing the same songs? Listen to birds on the play yard. How do their songs differ?

• Take a tape recorder along on a sound hunt. Record some of the sounds the children hear. Later, back in the room, see if children can tell where they were and identify the recorded sounds.

• Make your own *One Afternoon* or *One Morning* books. For a class *One Afternoon* book, each child can select a sound source to illustrate and/or write about. Or each child could make her or his own book of neighborhood sounds.

• Make the home-school connection. Send home Tear-Out Sheet 3 at the end of this chapter, which asks parents to help their children make a record of sounds in their home. Give children booklets made of plain paper stapled between two pieces of construction paper titled "Sounds in the Kitchen," "Home Sounds I Like the Best," or "Night Sounds."

◆ Specific sound games can be used during transition times, such as while waiting for lunch or a visitor.

• "What Is It?" Select three listeners and a sound maker. Ask the listeners to stand with their backs to the sound maker. The sound maker makes a sound with some object—perhaps a bell, a tone block, or another noisemaker. The three listeners then guess what made the sound. Ask the four players to each select another player to take their place, and repeat the game until all the children have had a turn.

Some noisemakers that require the sound maker to decide how to make sounds are

cellophane paper to crumble

a box of rocks or a container of rice, sugar, or sand

metal pie plates

metal cookie sheets

foil

springs

tools

coconut shells

- "Where Is It? Obtain a kitchen timer, and set it for a few seconds. One child hides the timer while the others cover their eyes. When the timer goes off, the children guess where it is hidden. Make sure each child gets a chance sometime to hide the timer.

◆ Activities can be added to a listening center or manipulative game area.

Montessori designed a series of wooden cylinders, all of the same size, with various materials enclosed in each cylinder. Two held sand; two, salt; two, pebbles; two, dried beans; and two, metal pins. Children were to develop the ability to match the two containers holding the same type of material.

You can replicate Montessori's original sound makers by filling pill bottles. Pairs of bottles could contain salt, sand, paper clips, rice, or any thing else that will make a sound when shaken. Securely tape the lids on the bottles, and cover the outside with opaque tape. Children can match the bottles containing the same material by themselves or do so with a partner.

◆ Extend children's ability to listen to specific sounds by creating a rhythm band. Purchase a few good instruments such as tone blocks, rhythm sticks, a step xylophone, bells, and good drums. Introduce the children to one instrument at a time, and for a specific purpose. For instance, they may take turns accompanying a song with the beat of a drum or rhythm sticks.

Practice with playing bells, sand blocks, and other instruments until children are familiar with all the instruments and the sounds they make. You might ask children which instruments they would choose to accompany parts of songs. For instance, they might suggest using sand blocks to accompany singing the song "Scraping Up Sand, Shiloh, Shiloh," or bells to accompany singing "Twinkle, Twinkle, Little Star."

As children explore the instruments ask them

- How many of the instruments make a striking sound?

- Which produce ringing sounds?

- What makes scraping sounds?

- How can the instruments be used to produce long, short, or smooth sounds?

A full band, with each child playing an instrument, is the end result. Make a video of the children's band. Listening to and viewing the video will permit children to evaluate their playing and gain skills in listening.

- Having created their own band, children will be ready to listen to CDs, tapes, and records of performances by musicians. A taped segment of a popular opera, musical, or symphony (perhaps one conducted by Billy McFarren) will offer children an appropriate listening experience. Visits from musicians, professionals, or older children who play a violin, viola, trumpet, or other instrument for the children expand children's interest in listening to music and their knowledge of how music is made.

- Listen to stories in music. With a background in listening to music, children will enjoy stories in music such as *Peter and the Wolf* by Sergei Prokofiev. You could read the story first, or use pictures of the story with the music. Finally, children will be able to listen to the sound story while making up their own pictures.

- Children enjoy listening to other types of music. They can listen to and march to the music of John Philip Sousa. Or they can listen to Camille Saint-Saëns' *Carnival of the Animals* and make up their own dance and movement to the story.

2. *Children Will Listen Actively*

◆ A number of games involve children in listening with purpose and for meaning. Some can be played during transition times; others are incorporated into group meetings.

- Play a form of "Simon Says." The teacher begins as the leader, standing before the group and saying, "Simon says put your hands on your head," and doing so. After the children are familiar with the game, the teacher then makes a statement but executes a different action. She may say, "Simon says stand up," and instead of standing, will sit down. Children can take turns being the leader.

- The "Silly Game" also requires children to listen with purpose and for meaning. The teacher gives a child two or three directions (the sillier the better) to follow in sequence while the others watch. She may say, "Give Vanessa a red crayon, shut the door, and sit on the floor." Children take turns following the directions. Once familiar with the game, children can lead.

◆ Extend children's ability to listen with purpose by asking them to respond to, and participate in, poems, stories, finger plays, and chants.

- Begin with poems. You might read "The Noble Duke of York," and have children respond rhythmically as if they were the noble duke. Other poems children can respond to rhythmically include

    "Little Nancy Etticoat"—children pretend to be the burning candle.

    "Humpty Dumpty"—after children are familiar with the rhyme, have them select one Humpty Dumpty to sit on a wall, and the rest can choose to be either a king's horse or man or woman to act out the rhyme. Have the horses and men and women decide ahead of time how they will put Humpty back together again so the action is controlled.

    "Hickory, Dickory Dock"—with their hands, children pretend to be mice climbing the clock.

- Using big books of poems or nursery rhymes that children are very familiar with, you could occasionally insert a wrong word as you read. Saying "Jack and Jill went up the stairs" lets children catch you in a mistake. They can even point to the word *hill* in the big book or chart and show you your error.

- Play "Drumbeats." You'll need several small drums, either purchased or made by the children. One child is the leader and beats a number of times on his or her drum. The other children listen and then repeat the exact number of beats. Children take turns leading the drumming.

◆ When asked what listening is, children often say, "It's when you sit still and look at the teacher." But listening with purpose is more than just sitting still or playing listening games.

Children can learn to listen with purpose to each other, their teachers, and visitors to their group.

- Children can listen to another child tell about accomplishing a task. One child may tell the others how she or he

     followed a map and found the school office

     solved the problem of joining two pieces of wood together to make a bed for the housekeeping area

     completed a painting

     found information about cats and dogs

- News is shared daily. During the opening meeting teachers will describe the plans for the day and any changes that will occur. They will also have news to share. Some news may be close to children—a teacher is leaving to have a baby—or more distant—there was a recent flood in a nearby community.

     Children will have news to share as well. They sometimes think that sharing news means they have to tell about something new—new shoes, new clothing, or a new toy. Children can be taught that news does not mean something new, but rather is a report of a recent event.

     The audience is helped to listen by thinking of questions to ask the speaker, or ideas that they have to extend those of the speaker. Teachers can prompt, "What else would you like to know?" "What do you think about it?" "Have you ever found your way using a map?"

- Children will also listen with purpose to experts and authorities in various fields. Prior to a field trip to a clothing store, one class listed the questions they had about how clothing is made and how the store functioned. The chart listing the questions was cut apart, and teams of children were each given a question to ask. When the store manager answered the question, the team was responsible for remembering the answer. Some made notes with invented spelling, and others drew sketches on their clipboards to help them remember. Back in the classroom another chart was made listing the answers to the questions.

     Prior to a visit from a veterinarian who was going to talk about dogs and cats, children listed their questions. Again, each child or group of children was given a question to ask and the duty to record the answer.

- Ask children to listen to stories, music, rhymes and chant with a purpose.

Teach children a new song using the technique of "My Turn, Your Turn." You can introduce the new song by spontaneously singing it several times during the day. You might introduce the song during morning group meeting, or sing it during center time. During music time, sing it again. Then tell the children it will be your turn, then their turn. Sing the first refrain; then point to them and have the group, with your help, sing the next refrain. You could divide the group into those who are wearing something red, or who have tie shoes, and only that group listens to you sing one refrain and responds by singing the next.

You could introduce a new song to the children by asking them first to listen to the song. Then the next time you sing it, ask them to listen carefully so they can answer specific questions. For example, if you introduce "Go Tell Aunt Rhody," you might ask them to listen to find out what you are to tell Aunt Rhody. Or if you sing "Over in the Meadow," they need to listen to tell what the mother bird or the frog sings to her young.

Call and answer songs, or echo songs, help children listen and reproduce sounds they hear.

Children could make up rhymes containing riddles. Start by telling them a riddle: "I rhyme with duck. Some people ride in me. What am I?" Or "I rhyme with chair. It's on our heads. What is it?" Then children take turns making up their own riddles and asking others to guess the answers.

3.   *Children Will Listen Critically*

Learning to listen critically enables children to respond with emotion and humor and to make critical judgments about what they hear.

◆   To develop critical listening, children must first be able to listen to understand a message, and be aware of what another is saying. Then they must filter the message, analyzing and evaluating it.

◆   Children listen critically as teachers read factual and informational books to find answers to their questions. One group became fascinated with a large, furry spider that spun a web in a corner of their room. Their questions about what kind of spider it was, what it would eat, and how it spun its web were answered as they listened to their teacher read books on spiders.

Draw children's attention to a variety of sounds. Perhaps children hear the wind whistling around the center building, a cricket singing in a tree, a baby crying, or the sounds of children laughing on the play yard. When you hear these, ask children how the sounds make them feel. Which sounds make them happy? Sad? Frightened?

Ask children to complete these sentences:

Some sounds are as quiet as . . .

Some sounds are as large as . . .

Sound sounds are as scary as . . .

Children can draw/paint or write their responses.

◆   Listening to poetry, songs, chants, and literature gives children the opportunity to evaluate the messages conveyed. The lovely poems of Langston Hughes—"Winter Sweetness," "Garment," or "City," found in *The Collected Poems of Langston Hughes* (Hughes, 1994)—stir up feelings and emotions. After reading "Winter Sweetness," ask children how they would feel if they were the maple sugar child living in a sugar house, its roof piled with snow. Or after reading "Garment," ask them what clothing they would weave from the clouds. And how do they feel at night when they go to bed in a city "hanging lights about its head," as Hughes writes in the poem "City"?

Ask children to paint, draw, or use collage or other art materials to portray their reactions to the poems.

- Children can be asked to judge what part of a story or picture they liked the best, which part frightened them or made them feel safe, or which part they liked the least. They can also be asked to recognize different points of view in stories. For instance, who in *The Little Red Hen* had the most sense?

- After reading stories, ask children what they thought of the major character. You might ask them if Peter Rabbit was wise to go back to Mr. McGregor's garden, or how they would feel lost in a store like Corduroy (Freeman, 1968). For other books, ask children which character was being silly, or which one was the smartest.

◇ **Documenting Children's Listening Skills**

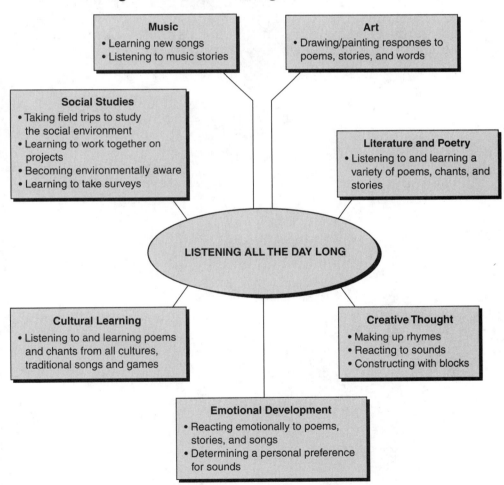

Date

Dear Families:

We are enjoying learning and listening to a variety
of songs and music in preschool. Such activity is not
only fun for children, but it helps them learn to
discriminate between sounds. They are gaining
auditory memory and learning to distinguish between
specific sounds, both skills that are necessary for
learning to read.

Do you remember a favorite song from when you were a
child? Would you please sing that song to your child
and tell him or her why it was your favorite? Ask your
child to sing along with you. If you can, you might
record you and your family singing together and send
the tape to school so we can enjoy the song as well.

Sincerely,

Date

Dear Parents:

Do you ever think of TV as a learning tool? By watching TV with your children you can help us achieve one of our goals—that of teaching children to listen critically.

After you and your children watch your favorite show together, perhaps *Shining Time Station*, *Teletubbies*, or *Barney*, talk about what you saw. Ask your children which characters they liked the best. What parts worried them? What would they do if they lived in *Shining Time Station*?

Let us know what TV shows your children enjoy with you at home so we can continue discussing these at school.

Thank you for your continuing support.

Sincerely,

Date

Dear Families:

We are going on walks to hunt for sounds in our
school and neighborhood. We will be asking children
to listen to the sounds of their home as well.

Will you and your child please fill the attached
booklet with pictures of things that make sounds in
your home? You and your child could draw these, or
cut pictures from magazines. At school we'll talk
about the booklets.

Sincerely,

Date

Dear Parents:

Tonight the story of _____ will be on Channel _____ at _____ p.m. We have read the story of _____ many times in class. Will you please watch the show with your children so we can discuss how the TV version of the story is the same as, and how it is different from, the version we read in class?

Thank you for working with us in developing children's critical listening skills.

Sincerely,

The Sounds and Patterns of Language
Developing Phoneme Awareness and Phonics

───────────── **FOR THE TEACHER** ─────────────

◇ **What You'll Need to Know**

Unlike knowledge children construct for themselves—ideas and concepts—developing awareness of the individual sounds of letters involves social knowledge. Social knowledge is arbitrary. We call one of the things we sit on *chair*. The name *chair* is social knowledge. This name is not constructed by children; it is told to them.

Chairs differ from each other not only in name but in style in differing cultures. In different cultures chairs take on very different forms and names, yet all chairs, regardless of name or form, have one thing in common—they are designed for one person to sit on. This concept or idea is the knowledge children must construct or discover for themselves.

Likewise, the names of letters and their sounds are social knowledge. These differ in each culture but serve the same purpose or function—that of forming the sounds we speak and read. Children can pick up some knowledge of letter names and their corresponding sounds informally as they live. Thus, the first step is to surround children with the sounds and patterns of language. Listening to poetry, chants, rhymes, and songs, and making up their own rhyming chants and songs, familiarize children with the sounds of letters and words, of alliteration and rhyme.

Because learning the sounds of letters is social knowledge, teachers need to introduce letter-sound correspondence intentionally. Even so, the more meaningful the context in which children are taught letter-sound correspondence, or symbol-sound correspondence in nonalphabetic language, the more fruitful the experience.

Further, it's not necessary to teach children every phoneme, letter-sound, or in the case of nonalphabetic language, symbol-sound. Once children get used to the idea that letters or symbols have sounds, they are able to learn others as they listen, read, and use invented spelling. Phonemes such as /f/, /m/, and /s/, which are easy to pronounce by themselves, and unvoiced consonants like /t/ and /p/ are the ones teachers often include as they develop children's literacy skills.

◇ **Concepts Key to Developing Phoneme Awareness and Phonics**

Awareness of the sounds and patterns of language begins with learning the names of letters. After letter names are learned, phonemic awareness includes

- the ability to detect rhyme and alliteration

- phonological memory

- the ability to break down and manipulate spoken words and isolate sounds in words

◇ **Goals and Objectives**

Children will be able to detect rhyme and alliteration by recalling and saying chants, poems, and songs, and by filling in rhyming words in repetitive and alliterative poems and stories.

Children will use their knowledge of letter names to learn letter sounds. They will be able to recognize and say the letter sounds of familiar consonants and recognize onsets and rimes.

◇ What You'll Need

A background understanding phoneme awareness and phonics and their relation to learning to read will be helpful. Contact the following resources for information about phoneme awareness.

ERIC Clearinghouse on Reading, English, and Communication
www.eric.gov or 1 800 LET-ERIC

The Reading Genie offers valuable information on teaching phonemes, including the article "Making Friends with Phonemes."

www.auburn.ed/~murraba/phon

Additionally, you'll need

- a variety of books, poems, nursery rhymes, chants, and songs
- art supplies, mural paper, collage materials, markers, crayons, and paints

◇ The Home-School Connection

Phoneme awareness is usually of high concern to parents. You can help alleviate their concerns by using the letter on the tear-out sheet at the end of this chapter.

◇ Evaluating and Assessing Children's Phoneme Awareness and Phonics

Observe and interview children to determine their level of phoneme awareness.

- Observe during center time and record children's interest in the sounds and names of letters. Note which children were involved and how.

- As you read poems, leave out the rhyming words at the ends of sentences. Note, and later record, which children were able to fill in the words correctly.

   Using the same technique, interview individual children and note which ones are able to complete the rhyme and with what degree of efficiency and correctness, which ones are just beginning to rhyme words, and which ones are not.

- Keep a list of nursery rhymes, songs, chants, and finger plays that children know as a group at the beginning, middle, and end of the school year. Interview individual children and ask them to recite a poem, chant, and finger play at the beginning, middle, and end of the year.

- Determine children's knowledge of letter-sound associations (phonemes) by interviewing individuals. Show children a variety of letters, perhaps plastic or wooden ones. Select consonants that are familiar to the group. Have children pick a letter, then say its name and sound. Record how many phonemes each child knows.

- Note and record children's use of invented spelling in their art and other work. This will give you an indication of how they are using phonemes. For instance, a child may write and say, "This is my name," demonstrating no use of phonemes. She may write a *Col* and say, "This is my name, *Claire*," demonstrating some knowledge of letter-sounds. Or she may write *Claire,* demonstrating more accurate use of phonemes.

FOR THE CHILDREN

1. *Children Will Detect Rhyme and Alliteration*

By recalling and saying chants, poems, and songs, by filling in rhyming words in repetitive and alliterative poems and stories, children will become familiar with rhyme and alliteration.

◆   Poetry, nursery rhymes, chants, and songs enchant children. Filling their days with every kind of rhyming verse not only delights them, but gives them necessary practice in learning to hear, listen to, and recognize the sounds and patterns of language. For fun,

whisper, sing, or shout a poem

sit on a poetry rug

recite a poem whenever you feel like it and encourage children to do the same

have a special poetry chair or cushion

Nursery Rhymes

It's the nonsense and fun of nursery rhymes that hold great appeal for young children. Select rhymes that do not denigrate any racial or ethnic group, that portray both boys and girls in action, and that are not ageist.

• Repeat the chant of Humpty Dumpty over and over again. Once children chant with you, stop and let them fill in the rhyming word: "Humpty Dumpty sat on a wall. Humpty Dumpty had a great . . . ."

Three- and four-year-olds can act out Humpty Dumpty. They can choose one child to be Humpty Dumpty, and as you recite the rhyme again, they decide to be either one of the king's horses or men who put Humpty together again. Before they do so, however, ask them to think how they will do this so Humpty is not swamped with unwanted help.

Five-year-olds can make a mural of Humpty Dumpty. On a piece of mural paper have a committee paint a wall. Each child makes a Humpty Dumpty out of construction paper to sit on the wall. Complete the mural by having children write or dictate the answer to the question "Why did Humpty fall?" Title the mural "Why Humpty Dumpty Fell."

• Read "Hickory, Dickory Dock," stopping for children to fill in the rhyming words. They can stand and pretend to be clocks, making the motion of a mouse running up them and clapping when the clock strikes one and the mouse runs down again.

• "Jack and Jill" is a familiar rhyme. But do your children know all the verses? Obtain the complete Jack and Jill rhyme—one source is *Ring-a Ring O' Roses and a Ding, Dong Bell* (Marks, 1977). After children are familiar with the rhyme, they can choose to be either Jack or Jill and act out the motions to the complete rhyme.

- Five-year-olds can complete the rhyme "Pancake Day."

Pancake Day

Great A, little a
This is a pancake day;
Throw the ball low,
Those that come after
May sing heigh-ho!

Ask them to write or dictate a poem for the letter *B*. You might begin with:

Great B, little b
This is a bouncing ball day.

Children would complete the rhyme and on another day write a poem for Great *C*, little *c*, and so on.

- When children are familiar with many Mother Goose rhymes, they can play a guessing game. One child chooses a character in a favorite rhyme and acts out the role before the group. The group tries to identify who the character is and then recites the rhyme.

Poetry

Every type of poetry appeals to children—traditional, rap, and everything in between. They enjoy the rhythm, cadence, and interesting sounds and words.

- Throughout the ages children have listened to the poetry of Eugene Field, collected in *Poems of Childhood* (1904). Read his "The Gingham Dog and the Calico Cat." Do children know what gingham and calico are? Provide some sample scraps. Look at the two materials and have children tell you how they are different. Using the gingham and calico, paper, paste, and markers or crayons, let children draw their ideas of the poem.

- Don't forget the power of the classical poetry of Robert Louis Stevenson, found in *A Child's Garden of Verses* (1905). When children are swinging, recite "The Swing," which begins "How do you like to go up in a swing, Up in the air so blue?" And when it rains, chant his poem "Rain."
    Examine shadows. Go outside and see who can make the biggest shadow. Play shadow tag; the person who is "it" tags others by stepping on their shadows. Then go back inside and read Stevenson's poem "My Shadow" that begins "I have a little shadow that goes in and out with me."

- Read Hughes's "April Rain Song" in *The Collected Poems of Langston Hughes* (1994), which starts with the line "Let the rain kiss you," and his poem "Garment," about clouds weaving a shawl. Both are lovely to introduce to children. His "The Kids in School With Me" about the Spanish, Chinese, Jewish, Polish, Russian, and African-America kids sitting in front of, behind, and across from the narrator—"Just American kids together—the kids in school with me"—unites children of different racial and ethnic backgrounds. Or look for the poetry of Eloise Greenfield and Maya Angelou to introduce children to other African-American poets.

- The humorous poems of Shel Silverstein, found in *Where the Sidewalk Ends* (1974), are equally enjoyed. Five-year-olds might make up their own silly poems in the fashion of the baby-sitter who thought she was hired to sit on the baby. Children find delight in the poems of Jack Prelutsky as well.

- How about starting a poetry corner? Just a small corner or nook can be set aside. Print a familiar poem and post it on a chart in the nook along with the book of poems.

    You could add collage materials for children to create their own garment of clouds, or drawing and writing materials for them to draw or write about how high they can swing.

◆ Hearing the same rhymes over and over, acting them out, and drawing their ideas of the rhymes will enable children to memorize a number of rhymes. This gives them pride and feelings of competence.

- During transition times children can informally, together or in a group, recite the rhymes they know.

- If your center or school holds parent nights or school assemblies and asks your class to participate, you can have your children demonstrate their love of the sounds and patterns of language by informally and spontaneously reciting the poems and rhymes they love. No need to rehearse. Children will simply do what they do when in their own classroom. Impress the audience even more by asking the children to select the poems or rhymes to recite.

◆ Make the home-school connection. About once a month make a booklet of poems, chants, and rhymes the children have enjoyed or written themselves. Duplicate these so each child can take home a booklet of "September Poems and Rhymes." Attach the letter on the tear-out sheet at the end of this chapter, which gives parents suggestions for using children's poetry books at home. Make certain these booklets are translated into the home languages of the children.

◆ Start making up rhymes and asking children to do the same.

- Begin by making up chants to go along with children's motions and activities. For example, when children are pounding clay, you could chant,

Push, pound, push, pound
Your hands go up and then go down.

When they are swinging, chant,

Swing high, swing low
Where will you go?

When they are playing in sand, chant,

Shake, shake,
Sift, sift,
Soft and gritty sandy land.

- Start children making their own rhymes by saying

  > Ms. Bunny likes bread and . . . . (honey)
  >
  > Mr. Sam likes bread and . . . . (jam)

  or

  > A cat is wearing a . . . (hat)
  >
  > A duck is driving a . . . (truck)
  >
  > A car is traveling . . . . (far)

- Make a collection of words that rhyme. One kindergarten class studied shoes and then started a chart titled "Rhyming Shoe." The words the children listed were *foo, boo, glue.* Next they studied socks and made a "Rhyming Sock" chart with the words *dock, lock, knock,* and *block.*

- Play rhyming riddles with 4- and 5-year-olds. You can say

  > I went to the farm and saw a cow. The cow said . . . (children fill in a rhyming word).
  >
  > I have shaggy hair, I must be a . . . (bear).

- During transition times, play "The Ship Is Loaded With." Say the ship is loaded with dogs. Children then add things to load the ship that rhyme with dogs such as logs, fogs, and togs, or say the ship is loaded with cheese, and the children add peas, fleas, and so on.

- Play "Rapping Rabbits" and have children make up rapping songs with rapping rabbits. You could start by saying

  > One rapping rabbit, went out to play.
  > The second rapping rabbit said what a fine day.
  > The third rapping rabbit said let's play.
  > The fourth rapping rabbit said ok.
  > Roof, roof, roof, rapped the neighbor's dog and
  > the fifth rapping rabbit said let's hop away.

  Have children make up their own rapping rabbit verses.

◆ Poems that are based on alliteration are helpful in introducing children to the sounds of initial consonants.

◆ Read some of *Aster Aardvark's Alphabet Adventures* (Kellog, 1987). The comical choruses and catchy cadences found in this book are a fun way of introducing children to alliteration and initial sounds of letters. After reading this or other poems with alliteration, 5-year-olds can make up their own alliterative poems.

◆ Try some tongue twisters. Dr. Bruce Murray, *The Reading Genie* (*http://www.auborn.ed./"morraba/* or *www.The Reading Genie*) suggests introducing tongue twisters like *N*obody was *n*ice to *N*ancy's *n*eighbor *N*ick, but he was *n*ever *n*asty.

Once children learn a tongue twister, give them practice in splitting the initial sounds by talking like a puppet: N-obody was n-ice to N-ancy, and so on.

2. *Children Will Learn Letter Sounds*

Use children's knowledge of letter names to help them learn letter sounds. They will be able to recognize and say the letter sounds of familiar consonants and recognize onsets and rimes.

Learning letter-sound correspondence is a difficult task for young children. The more letter names they know, and the more teaching is embedded in a meaningful context, the easier it will be for children to learn letter-sound correspondence.

◆ Begin introducing letter-sound correspondence with one of the most meaningful things children have—their names.

- Every time, or nearly every time, you write children's names on their artwork or stories or on a chart, say the names of the letters: "Helen, this is the *H*. Your name begins with the same letter as Harry Potter's name."

  Or you could say, "Look—your name begins with *N*. It's the same sound that begins the words *nice, nose,* and *nail.* Can you hear the *N?*" Frame the letter you are talking about with your fingers so children can see that their name is comprised of individual letters, and that these letters have sounds.

- Make each child a name booklet. Staple a couple of pieces of paper between two sheets of construction paper. Print the child's name on the cover. Underline the beginning letter and write the letter on the cover as well. As children encounter or use words that begin with the same initial sound as their name, add these to their booklets. Children can also find pictures of things that begin with the same initial as their names to paste in their booklets. They can keep these booklets handy, in their cubbies or mailboxes.

- Play "Guess Who?" Pronounce the sound of the initial consonant of a child's name. Perhaps *s s s s.* Then ask, "Whose name am I thinking of?" Children, if they've heard the sound of the initial letter of their name frequently, will be able to guess, "It's me! I'm Susan."

◆ Use chart work or big books to introduce children to the sounds of letters that begin words.

- As you read a big book, frame initial letters with your hands. Say the letter name and its sound. Ask children to find the same letter on other pages, frame it with their hands, name it, and say the sound of the letter.

- Charts are useful in writing group invitations, thank-you notes, and news. One group of 4-year-olds received a bag of new balls of all sizes and colors. Together the children dictated the following news story to the teacher. She did some minor editing as the children told her what to write.

> New balls
> Red ones, small ones
> New balls.
> Big ones, blue ones
> Bouncing, bouncing, all day long.

The teacher pointed out the letter *b* in the title, said its sound, and asked children to find, frame, and say the name and sound of other *b*'s in the chart.

◆ Most effective of all is to teach letter sounds "while you're at it."

• While zipping up a child's coat, say, "Zipper—listen for the *z*. The letter *z* even sounds like a zipper."

• While buttoning a coat, say, "*B* is for button, hear the *b, b, b.*"

• While sipping juice through a straw, say, "Sipping, sipping, sipping—sipping starts with *s*. Listen to its sound."

• When writing a thank-you note to the firefighter who visited the class, point out the *f* that begins *fire* and *fighter,* and say its sound.

• When reading *Chicka, Chicka, Boom, Boom* (Martin & Archambault, 1989), say "Listen to the sound of the *b* in *boom, boom.*

• When printing a label for the block builders who asked for a sign saying "Do Not Knock Down," ask them to tell you what letter they think *do* begins with. Do the words *down* and *do* begin with the same sound and letter?

◆ Make a set of keyword cards. These, which integrate letter/keyword/picture, seem to help children remember letter names (Adams, 1998). You can make a set by drawing pictures of letters on cards. Make duplicate sets of cards and laminate them so children can play games with them. Children are adept at making up their own "card" games, or you can teach them to sort the cards by the shape of the letters, the letters they know, or those that are in their names, or to match like letters.

◆ Letter-sound games are enjoyed by children and are great for transition times when, for one reason or another, the children and you have to wait. You could try the following, or make up your own games to increase children's awareness of beginning sound, same-sounding, and different-sounding letters.

• Play "Same or Different." Ask children to listen to two words and tell whether they begin alike or begin with different letters. Say *tin* and *Tommy,* or *mat* and *mitten.* Then say *cat* and *mother.* Write the initial letters of the words on a chart, then say their names and sounds. After children catch on, add another word so two begin with the same letter and the third does not.

• Make a set of picture cards of words that begin with the same consonant. You might find pictures of a cat, car, card, can, cookie, and so on. Label the cards with the name of the object and its initial letter. Children can sort the cards, play with them, or match them with plastic or cut-out letter *c*'s from a box of alphabet letters. As they play with the cards, point out that the names of the objects begin with the same letter, *c*.

Next add another letter. A child in one group had gone to Disney Land on vacation. She came back with a small Mickey Mouse doll as a souvenir for each child. The children were delighted with the dolls. Picking up on their interest, the teacher pointed out that Mickey and Mouse begin with the same letter and sound, *m,* and asked what other things they could find in the room beginning with *m.* She listed their responses and made a second set of cards of objects that began with *m.*

Now children played with two sets of cards. They sorted the *c* cards and the *m* cards and played matching games they made up. As other occasions arose, the teacher added other letters to the cards. On a windy day she added the letter *w,* and when the apple tree outside their window began to blossom, she added the letter *b.* By the end of the year, the children were familiar with the letter names and sounds of the majority of the consonants.

◆   Move beyond listening to and learning rhymes and poems. Once children are familiar with rhyming words, introduce them to the idea of onsets and rimes. Onsets are the initial sounds of any consonants that precede vowels, such as the *c* in *cat,* the *h* in *hat,* and so on. Rimes consist of vowels and any consonants that come after the initial consonant. It is believed that awareness of onsets is key to phonemic awareness. In preschool and kindergarten, teachers can intentionally focus children's attention on onsets and rimes.

• Make a chart of the words in Seuss's *The Cat in the Hat* (1987), separating the onset from the rime, *at.* Some teachers use different color markers to differentiate the onset from the rime.

• Give children a rime, such as *in,* and ask them to make words by adding a letter in front of the rime. Start them with *p in,* writing the *p* and then the rime *in.* What other words do they know that rhyme with *pin*? Show them how only the onset differs in *tin, din, sin, win, fin,* and so on. Repeat when poems include common rimes such as *ake, all, ell,* and so on.

◆   A word about the letter of the week!

Some school systems institute a curriculum that consists of introducing children to a "letter of the week." Many teachers, finding this artificial, have kept records of the letter sounds children have learned through informal and more formal ways. After assessing the children, one kindergarten teacher noted that there were several consonants the children did not know. Instead of a "letter of the week," she found other ways to teach these to the children.

For example, one letter name and sound many children did not know was that of *w.* One day she brought in a little red wagon filled with objects and pictures of things beginning with *w.* She wrote "Little Red Wagon" on the chalkboard and the letter *w.* She asked children to pick objects out of the wagon, say their name, and name the letter they began with. Next, she took the chart listing children's names and asked them to find the letter *w* and say its sound in their names. Finally, each child was given a small paper paint can and a paintbrush and sent outside to write the letter *w* on the play yard. She explained that the children were gaining not just social knowledge of the letter *w,* but perceptual motor skills, the ability to think on their feet as they talked about something in the wagon, and social skills in learning to recognize their name and the names of their classmates.

◇ Documenting Children's Developing Phoneme and Phonic Awareness

A web documents the integrated nature of children's phoneme awareness.

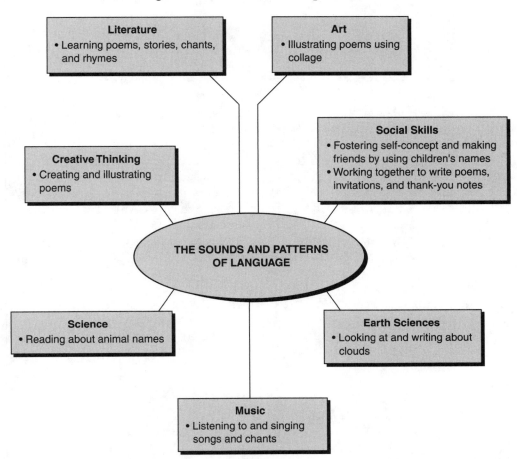

Literature
• Learning poems, stories, chants, and rhymes

Art
• Illustrating poems using collage

Social Skills
• Fostering self-concept and making friends by using children's names
• Working together to write poems, invitations, and thank-you notes

Creative Thinking
• Creating and illustrating poems

THE SOUNDS AND PATTERNS OF LANGUAGE

Science
• Reading about animal names

Earth Sciences
• Looking at and writing about clouds

Music
• Listening to and singing songs and chants

Date

Dear Parents:

Many of you have asked if your children will learn phonics while in our early childhood program. Although we will not drill your children in "phonics," they will become aware of letters and their sounds.

First, our program is filled with the sounds and patterns of language. Being able to hear and detect rhyme and alliteration is the first step in learning to discriminate letters and their sounds. Next, in the context of everyday events, we will introduce children to specific letters and their sounds.

You can support our work by reading poems to your children. Each month we will send home a booklet of poems and finger plays the class has learned for you and your children to enjoy together. Other poetry books can be borrowed from our lending library or your local library.

You might

- collect poems from birthday and other greeting cards

- read nursery rhymes and poetry you enjoyed as a child

- make up rhymes as you go along

You can also support your children's awareness of letter sounds by pointing these out. Point out letter sounds that have some personal meaning to your children. For example, you can point out the *M*'s in the names Mickey and Minnie Mouse, which have the same sound as Michele's name.

Sincerely,

6

The Symbol Makers
Developing Awareness of and Making Print

FOR THE TEACHER

◇ What You'll Need to Know

"Look, Mommy," says 3-year-old Katie showing her mother a scribble she has just completed. "I wrote a letter for Grandma. It says I love you!" When children are surrounded by print and observe the adults around them reading and writing, they become aware of print and its function.

Observing, children learn that there is a difference between print and pictures. Four-year-old Juan, when asked to write his name, drew a series of circles and lines in a linear fashion across the paper. When asked to draw himself riding on a horse, he moved the crayon quickly back and forth across the paper saying, "I ride fast, faster, and faster."

The early childhood curriculum supports children's understanding and use of print. As children play at writing, they scribble, print letter-like shapes, or form cursive-like markings, imitating the adults they see. These early scribbles or writing may or may not be intended to carry a message. Often writing is mixed in with a painting or a drawing, but it usually is the picture that carries the meaning, not the writing.

From 3 to 5 years of age, children's scribble writing may include random symbols or letters, or strings of letters. By 5 years of age or so, children may write individual letters that represent a sound, such as *m,* or a syllable, like *mk* for *milk,* beginning to relate letters to speech segments. They may print a string of letters and ask, "What does this word say?" demonstrating their awareness that print stands for something in reality. Conventional words, such as their own name, may appear in their play writing and drawings.

◇ Concepts Key to Awareness of Print and Printing

- Both print and pictures are used to communicate messages.
- Print differs from pictures because it holds information that cannot be conveyed through pictures.
- There are many different kinds of, and uses for, print.
- Children can print to communicate through the written word.

◇ Goals and Objectives

Children will use drawings, scribbles, and writing to convey messages.

Children will use a variety of drawing tools and art materials as a means of communication through drawings and print.

Children will demonstrate that they can gain meaning from their own scribbles, drawings, and writing and from those of others.

Children will develop the skills of printing the letters in their names and other letters.

◇ What You'll Need

To begin, you'll need a print-rich environment. Not only is print used to label displays, but it is used with purpose and for a function. Obtain a copy of Catherine E. Loughlin and Mavis Martin's book *Supporting Literacy: Developing Effective Learning Environ-*

ments (1987), from Teachers College Press, New York, and a copy of Susan Neuman, Carol Copple, and Sue Bredekamp's book *Learning to Read and Write* (2000) from the National Association for the Education of Young Children, Washington, DC. These books show you the possibilities for using print throughout the room and school building to foster children's awareness and use of print.

Next, you'll need the following:

- a variety of writing tools and all kinds of paper. Make blank booklets consisting of a couple of pieces of paper stapled between two construction paper covers and blank journals.

- a writing center or area that includes a computer.

- books and written materials of every kind throughout the room and in a library area.

- an assortment of art prints. These can be obtained from your local library or art museum or from magazines and newspapers.

- plastic, wooden, and rubber stamp letters; card sets of sandpaper and printed letters, both upper- and lowercase.

- stick and circle pretzels.

A number of Web sites offer resources for teachers and parents.

For information for parents and teachers on early literacy development, including drawing and learning to print, contact the ERIC Clearinghouse on Elementary and Early Childhood Education.

ericeece@uiuc.edu

For parents, obtain a copy of *Emergent Literacy: What Young Children Can Learn About Reading and Writing Before They Go to School.*

www.edc.org/FSC/NCIP/Tour/Intro

◇ **The Home-School Connection**

Parents' involvement in their children's learning to write is critical. You might use the letters on the tear-out sheets at the end of this chapter to let parents know what they can do to develop children's awareness of print and how to print.

◇ **Assessing and Evaluating Children's Awareness of Print**

Use the checklist on Tear-Out Sheet 4 (p. 134) to observe and record children's awareness of print.

———————————— **FOR THE CHILDREN** ————————————

1. *Children Will Use Art as a Means of Communication*

The ability to print stems from children's early scribbles. Thus, children are encouraged to express themselves through their scribbles, drawings, paintings, and other artworks.

◆   Those seemingly aimless scribbles, circles, lines, and forms are the building blocks for children's graphic knowledge. All of the lines, circles, and forms children need to use to form print are found in their scribbles.

Three-Year-Olds

• Make certain that children have large sheets of newsprint and chunky crayons that won't easily break or markers available to them at all times.

• Provide lots and lots of newsprint because threes get pleasure from moving and making marks at the same time. Their joy has no boundaries, so be sure it's okay for them to scribble off the paper and on the table.

• You don't need to save all the scribbles or put children's names on them. Select samples, however, to put in children's portfolios, or to show parents the progress they are making in controlling scribbles and the importance of these controlled scribbles. See the figure on the next page.

• When talking to children about their scribbles, focus on what they are doing: "You moved your arm all across the paper"; "These marks go up and down, up and down just like your hand did."

• Threes can scribble with paint as well. Two or three colors of paint, large easel paper, and brushes that can be grasped by a 3-year-old's hand are all that's required.

Four-Year-Olds

• Fours still need lots of newsprint and freedom to scribble, but they will begin to name their scribbles. As they scribble, some line or shapes will remind them of something, and they'll say, "See, here's my duck." When they do so, you can write the title on their scribble, along with their name.

• Because fours assign meaning to their scribbles, they can use additional drawing tools that will permit them to express themselves in more detail. Provide other kinds of paper and materials to use for drawing—construction paper of various colors and crayons, markers, and pens. Add another color or two to the easels.
  Extend drawing time to the out-of-doors. Take large chunky chalk outside so children can scribble and draw on the play yard. Hang large mural paper on the school fence or building along with a six-pack of paints so children can paint outside. A bucket of crayons and large newsprint on a concrete pour or picnic table encourage more drawing.

• Once children start to name their scribbles, you know they are assigning meaning to them. Picking up the child's cue—"This is s stork. See the long legs?"—ask questions relating to the child's idea and how she or he expressed it through drawing or painting: "Where did you see a stork?" "The legs are really long. How did you use your brush to make them so long?"

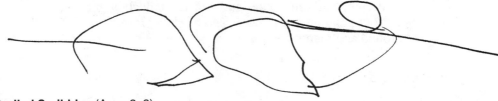

Uncontrolled Scribbles (Ages 2–3)

Controlled Scribbles (Ages 3–4)
(Scribble writing at bottom of page)

Elaborated Scribbles (Ages 4–5)
(Letter-like scribbles appear)

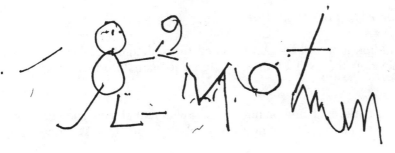

Schematic Drawings (Ages 5–7)
(Writing incorporated into pictures)

Don't force conversation on children or force them to name their drawing. When asked to "tell about your painting," one 4-year-old told the teacher, "It's just a design, that's all—a design." You can talk about the color in a child's drawing: "Your painting is all yellow and bright." Or the lines: "This line goes round and round and round the paper."

Five-Year-Olds

Five-year-olds now use schema, symbols such as a circle to represent a head or a sun, lines to stand for arms and legs, and a rectangle to represent a house. Their drawings and paintings seem to carry more meaning than those of 3- and 4-year-olds. Using invented spelling, fives will write their names, label things in a drawing or painting, and give it a title.

- Introduce children to the idea of portraits. Show them portraits of children. They can then draw or paint

  a self-portrait using a mirror

  a portrait of a friend who serves as a model

  a portrait of their favorite character in a story

- Themes about "I," "me," and "myself" appeal to the egocentrism of fives. Ask them to draw or paint about themselves.

How do they look when they jump rope?—"Where are your arms when you jump? Where are your feet? What do your knees do?"

How do they look when they skip?—"How do your feet move? Which one goes first? What do you do with your arms when you skip?"

After the drawings are completed, have children title them and explain them in writing using invented spelling or tell about them.

2. *Children Will Gain Meaning From Print*

◆ Daily, young children look at and gain meaning from pictures. Still, they do not automatically develop the skill of using pictures to gain information or solve problems.

- With very young children, begin picture reading with real objects and events before asking them to interpret meaning from symbols or pictures. When working with 3-year-olds,

  name the object or event—"This is an eggbeater."

  talk about what it is used for—"We're going to use it to beat egg whites to make cookies."

  relate the object to children's previous experiences—"Does your mom or dad use an eggbeater? What does it look like?"

- Enter into a dialogue with a child about things you see in a picture. Pick photographs or pictures of children at work or play, animals, machines, or other things and events children have experienced.

Ask, "What do you see?" If children are not familiar with "reading" pictures, name things in the picture: "Here is a horse. There's the barn." The next time you look at a picture in a book or a photograph, ask them to name the things they see.

The next stage in picture reading is to interpret what they see. Ask, "What is happening?" "Why did it happen?" "What will she do now?" "Do you think she did the right thing?" "What would you do?"

- Take candid photos of children as they work and play. Using digital photos make booklets or scrapbooks. Mount another set of photos on a mural for the hall or entrance way. Title the booklet and the mural. Print children's names under the photos with a sentence or phrase describing what they were doing, saying, and learning at the time.

 Make a duplicate set to keep on a table for children to handle and sort through. As they do so,

 name the children in the photos

 talk about what they were doing

 ask children what they remember of the activity and how they felt at the time

- Present older children with a reproduction of a painting. These can be obtained from your local library. Show the painting to the group, and tell them who the artist is and where she or he lived and when. Then ask children to name the work of art. After they do so, tell them the name the artist selected and why.

 On another day, perhaps with another painting or picture, ask children to begin a story about the painting, with each child taking a turn in developing the story.

 Another game is to find things in the painting. One child can start and name one thing she or he sees in the painting. Each child, in turn, names something else in the painting, trying to name or see a secret thing.

◆ Use wordless books for picture reading. Examples of wordless books for young children to "read" include the following:

Bang, M. (1980). *The grey lady and the strawberry snatcher.* New York: Four Winds.

dePaola, T. (1978). *Pancakes for breakfast.* New York: Harcourt Brace Jovanovich.

Hutchins, P. (1971). *Changes.* New York: Macmillan.

Spier, P. (1997). *Peter Spier's rain.* New York: Doubleday.

Write down the stories the children tell to use as library books, and have them illustrate their own stories.

◆ Displays of children's work and their products help them understand that meaning is conveyed through print and pictures. These displays also allow children to reflect on their experiences, organize their thinking, and use printed language as a means of communication. Displays also serve to inform the school staff, parents, and the community about how young children learn, grow, and develop.

 Use large bold letters that can be read from a distance to label the board. Keep titles brief and use smaller letters to label parts of the display. Label the work not only with children's names, but with what they said and did while creating the work. Other labels can explain the experience or activities that led to the creation of the display.

- Bulletin boards are one form of display. Those that children can "do something" with are most enjoyed.

    When children return from a walking field trip to find textures inside and outside of their building, a bulletin board titled "Touch Me If You Will" could be created. On the board you could mount and label bits and pieces of tile, wood, concrete block curtains, plants, leaves, acorns, and other things discovered on the trip for children to touch, feel, and talk about.

    One group of 5-year-olds released ladybugs in their garden. They then painted a mural of the garden, hiding ladybugs throughout. The board was titled "How Many Ladybugs Can You Find?" Children spent much time talking about, finding, and counting the ladybugs they each had hidden in the mural.

    An alphabet bulletin board can be created. Select a few letters, perhaps consonants the children are learning. Cut these out of light cardboard or felt mounted on cardboard. Using pushpins, place the letters at the bottom of the board. On the board above the letters, place objects or pictures that begin with these letters. Children then pin the letter with the correct object.

- Other displays are three dimensional. You might use any of the following to hold a display:

    sturdy cardboard boxes

    shelves

    a shelf of wood or particleboard attached underneath a bulletin board

    a card table that can be folded and put away.

  Some examples of displays are

- photographs taken during a trip to the fire station, a piece of fire hose, drawings of the firefighters, and fire trucks children have constructed of blocks or from boxes

- different types of plants they found on the play yard

- rocks found on the play yard and around the neighborhood, categorized in clear containers, along with photos of children finding them. Add a magnifying glass with the direction "Look Closer" to involve children.

◆ Obviously, the best way children learn to gain meaning from print is through the use of books.

3. *Children Will Develop Skills in Printing*

They will be able to print some of the letters in their names and other letters.

◆ You serve as a powerful model for children. Because they adore you, they will copy what you do and say and how you behave. Take advantage of this by letting children see you as you write so they can model after you.

- Perfect your own manuscript printing. When you print, use capitals and lowercase letters.

- Talk with individual children about how letters are formed. As you write a child's name on his or her painting, say, "*A* is the first letter of your name. It's made with a slanting line, then . . ." Or talk about how letters are made when you do other writing:

- Write a functional label for the room such as "Paper Towels Here!"

- Print a sign for children's block building—"Do Not Disturb."

- Take dictation from children—they might tell you the questions they want to ask a visitor, what they will look for on a field trip, or what they learned about the cafeteria.

- Write the title of a child's painting.

◆ Observe children and take every opportunity to show them how letters are formed. When you see them struggling to print their names or a message on their painting, you can show them how the letters are formed. Be sensitive and careful, however. No child interested in painting an impression of a rabbit wants to be interrupted and shown how to print his or her name.

◆ Provide ways for children to practice printing.

- Have models of letters. A set or two of letter cards, with upper- and lowercase letters, are useful in the writing, library, manipulative, and sociodramatic play areas.

- Use an overhead with transparencies for children to practice printing. At first they'll just enjoy scribbling and watching their reflection on the screen.

    After they tire of the novelty, show one or two children at a time how to print letters. You might begin by practicing circles, showing them how to shape the letters that are formed with a circle or partial circle. Do the same with letters formed with straight, slanted, or curved lines.

    Early on, children recognize the letters that begin their names, and you might start with these. Direct their attention to the screen and enlarge the writing. Have them practice printing, but vary the practice. One day ask children to write only letters that are made from a circle or part of a circle. On another day, only letters made with lines. Make sure all children have turns with the overhead.

- Children also enjoy practicing printing on small chalkboards. Provide a few chalkboards with different kinds of chalk and erasers on a table during choice time. Work with the children as they form letters.

- Take chunky chalk out on the play yard and let children practice printing their names or other letters in a larger form. Or give them small paper paint buckets and cheap paintbrushes to print in paint all over the play yard.

- As a special choice during center time, give children pretzels to form letters. Small groups of children can work at a table set with a piece of paper toweling and a plastic container holding a snack-size portion of stick and circle pretzels at each place. Taking turns, children can use the stick and circle pretzels to form the letters in their names or other letters. They can eat their creation as a snack anytime they wish.

- Use the Montessori method and give children letters made of sandpaper for them to trace with their fingers. Montessori also gave children trays lightly covered with sand for them to write letters in the sand.

- Letters can be formed from pipe cleaners as well.

◆   Most groups will include children who speak a language other than English. Take a look at the letters in their names and how they are just like those in English and how they differ. Some languages use accent marks, others such as Chinese and Korean are comprised of lines only, and eastern European languages use lines and circles in very different ways to form letters. Have children whose first language is not English show the others how to write in their languages.

◇ **Documenting Children's Learning to Print**

◆   Begin a literacy portfolio on each child in your class. In this folder keep samples of children's scribbles taken from the beginning, middle, and end of the school year. Include other samples that demonstrate achievement of specific skills such as scribble writing, letter formation, or printed words. Date each sample and make a note of particular achievements. At the end of the year, you'll have a compete picture of each child's progress.

◆   Create frequent displays of children's artwork and early printing. Label these so others learn how children begin the process of writing.

◆   Create a web to display. Include samples of children's writing as well as their drawings and paintings.

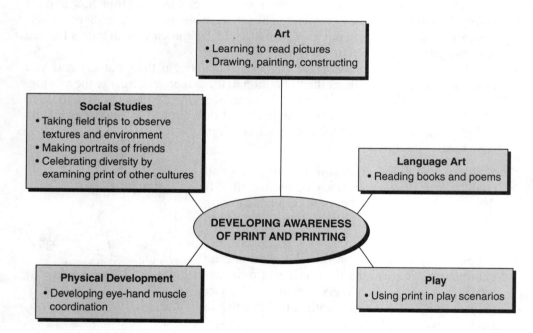

Date

Dear Families:

Your children will be bringing home a lot of
scribbles, drawings, and paintings this year. We want
you to know how important these are to children's
growth, development and learning.

First, children are learning to think as they
scribble, draw, and paint. Before drawing, they must
hold a thought, a feeling, or an idea in their mind,
then search for a way to express this through the
media, and finally develop the eye-hand-muscle
control to execute their feelings and ideas. This is
thinking in action.

Next, drawings and scribbles are important precursors
to learning to write. Children's beginning scribbles
are uncontrolled. As they develop control, they can
repeat marks such as the circles and straight lines
used in print. Around 4 years of age, children begin
to understand that their drawings carry a message and
will name them. When children have seen you writing,
and are surrounded with print, they'll begin to
incorporate print into their paintings.

The attached sheet illustrates how children's
scribbling develops into pictures and how the
development of print is incorporated into children's
drawings. This will help you follow your children's
artistic development as well as their development of
concepts of print.

Sincerely,

Date

Dear Families:

Here is a list of things you can provide for your
children so they can scribble, draw, paint, or write
at home.

They can scribble, draw, paint, or write on

- cardboard inserts that come in panty hose, shirts,
  or other packaged new clothing

- junk mail that has spaces to fill in

- the back of discarded computer paper

- small notepads from hotels and other businesses

- cardboard boxes

- paper bags cut open and laid flat

- newsprint

- discarded stationery and greeting cards

They can draw, paint, or write with

- chunks of chalk on the sidewalk

- water in plastic buckets and a paintbrush to take
  outside

- every type of crayon, marker, and pencil

In our lending library we also have backpacks
containing markers, pads of paper, and other drawing
supplies that you may check out.

Sincerely,

Date

Dear Families:

Children learn about print by watching you use print. You can foster children's awareness of print by doing the following:

- Read magazines with them. Look at the pictures, and ask what they see, what they think is happening, or how they would feel if they were the child in the picture.

- Read to children every night. Talk about what you read. Point out and read specific words. For example, if you're reading *Chicka, Chicka, Boom, Boom* by Bill Martin, point out "This word says 'boom.' Here's another 'boom.' Find another one."

- Read the children's section of the daily paper with your children.

- Consult the tv guide with your children in order to plan your tv watching for the evening or week.

- Wish through catalogs with your children.

- Read menus with your children.

There are many times during the day when you read and use print for many different purposes. Involve your children in as many of these times as possible.

Sincerely,

Checklist: Children's Awareness of Print

Name: _____   Date: _____

Art	Daily	Sometimes	Never
Uses art to convey ideas	_____	_____	_____
Includes letters in art	_____	_____	_____
Combines writing with art	_____	_____	_____
Uses left to right "writing"	_____	_____	_____
Incorporates single words in artwork	_____	_____	_____

Writing Play

	Daily	Sometimes	Never
Uses writing when playing	_____	_____	_____
Includes scribble writing	_____	_____	_____
Uses random symbols	_____	_____	_____
Writes single letters	_____	_____	_____
Writes single words	_____	_____	_____

7

Writing Throughtout the Day
Using Invented Spelling

─────────────── **FOR THE TEACHER** ───────────────

◇ **What You'll Need to Know**

Children who have had plenty of opportunity to express themselves on paper—scribbling, drawing, painting—are already on their way to becoming writers. They understand that print carries a different kind of message than pictures, and because they have this idea, they've begun to incorporate print in their drawings and paintings. They further demonstrate their knowledge of print when they ask to have their name or a story written on their drawings and paintings, or begin writing it themselves.

The early childhood program builds on children's initial ideas of the writing process and their eagerness to write. When children experiment with writing, or ask how a word is spelled, they are encouraged to invent their own spelling. According to the experts, children who are encouraged to invent their own spelling are better readers than children who are not encouraged to do so.

Doing so seems to develop children's abilities to reflect on their own thoughts, to organize their ideas and express themselves in print. When children try to spell words, they are required to think actively, form hypotheses, and learn to segment words into phonemes and syllables.

Encouraging invented spelling, however, does not mean that teachers never show children the correct way to spell a word. While encouraging children's functional and creative writing and free expression of ideas, teachers respond to their questions. When children ask, "Is this right?" or "How do you spell. . . ?" they are encouraged to sound out the word they want to spell before writing it. Or teachers might show children how to write the initial letter of the word they want to spell, or to look in one of the many different types of dictionaries around the room.

◇ **Concepts Key to Using Invented Spelling**

Children begin inventing spelling as they incorporate print into their paintings and drawings. Invented spelling involves the following:

- the understanding that the spoken word begins and ends with letters or blends of letters, has letters in between, and can be written

- knowledge of the alphabet, and awareness of graphemes, letter names, and sounds

- an understanding of the purpose and function of print, including the creative expression of ideas

◇ **Goals and Objectives**

Children will use writing for a purpose.

Children will express themselves daily through drawing, painting, and writing, including creative expression.

When told "just spell it the way it sounds," children will use letters or representations of letters, sounding out words when encouraged to do so and printing the letters they hear.

Children will begin to contribute to class stories and booklets.

◇ What You'll Need

You'll need an assortment of children's books. A list of appropriate books appears at the end of this book.

In addition, you'll need spaces and time for children to express themselves through picture and print, along with the materials and supplies to do so. Plenty of paper and tools for drawing, painting, and marking will be necessary both indoors and out-of-doors.

Several Web sites offer a great deal of information about invented spelling. You might forward some of this information to parents who question the use of invented spelling, or use it with your staff as you foster and assess children's writing and invented spelling.

The ERIC Clearinghouse on Reading, English and Communication offers numerous articles and resources on children's emergent literacy development and learning.

ericcs@indiana.edu; www.indianaedu/~eric_rec/ieo/bibs/spell.html

Parts of the document ED272922 86 *Invented Spelling and Spelling Development* by Elaine Lutz could be used to answer parents' questions about children's writing and the use of invented spelling.

◇ The Home-School Connection

Displays of children's writing enable parents to better understand how that writing develops.

- Display children's artwork. Include explanations of their initial attempts at writing.

- Along with photos of children on a field trip, doing field work, or working together on a project, include samples of their writing and explanations of it.

- Duplicate each child's work to send home in class booklets.

Keep parents informed about how they can assist in developing children's writing and invented spelling by sending home the letter on the tear-out sheet at the end of this chapter.

◇ Evaluating and Assessing Children's Writing Development and Use of Invented Spelling

Children's writing and use of invented spelling should be moving *from*

- using art to convey ideas

- pretending to write, using scribble writing to imitate cursive writing, stringing forms together that resemble letters

- including actual letters and pretend writing in their artwork to convey meaning

- writing single letters from rote

- asking "What does this say?"

and moving *to*

- writing beginning sounds of words: *t* for *truck*

- writing the beginning and ending sounds of words: *tk* for *truck*

- including middle sounds in written words: *trk* for the word *truck*

Their written or dictated ideas will be progressing

- from simple to complex, detailed, and complete

- from unformed to a semblance of story form, with beginnings and endings to their stories

FOR THE CHILDREN

1. *Children Will Use Writing for a Purpose*

◆   Rooms are arranged to encourage children to use writing for a purpose or function.

Clipboards

Keep clipboards and markers in centers of interest to encourage children to use print to record their work or collect data. Duplicate some recording sheets with lines and boxes to further motivate children.

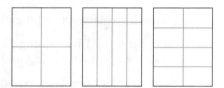

You might keep clipboards, plain and marked paper, markers, and crayons or pencils in various locations:

- next to the slide so children can record how many times they slide down

- on the science table so children can measure and record how fast the grass they planted is growing

- with books so children can record the books they've looked through

- with writing and art supplies so the clipboards are handy to take anywhere in the room

- available out of doors as well

Five-year-olds can conduct surveys using the clipboards. One class thought there was too much trash collecting around the play yard fence, so they decided to survey the school to find out what to do about it.

In groups of four or five, along with a supervising adult, they surveyed the center director, the cleaning crew, teachers, parents, and other children. Their results were analyzed, and they concluded that more trash cans needed to be placed around the play yard and that they would make signs to place outside the play yard to remind neighbors and others to put their trash in the containers.

Sign-Up Charts

Make sign-up charts so children can "sign up" for special projects or other centers:

- Keep a sign-up list titled "Easel Painters." Children sign up, writing their name. When they finish, they mark through their name, and then it's the next child's turn to paint.

- Keep the same type of sign-up list next to the computer station.

- When there's new play yard equipment, perhaps a new bike, children can sign up for their turn to use it.

Checkout Lists

Children enjoy signing their name to check out classroom materials. Checkout lists can be used for

- books
- computer programs
- pets
- plants
- videos
- class books created by the children

Appointment Lists

Four- and five-year-olds might keep appointment books, recording when they will play with a special friend or when they will build together, dig a fort in the sand, or paint on a mural together. Large calendars with a large space for each day allow children to record their "appointments."

What Do You Choose?

Other lists let children vote on their choices or preferences.

- After reading "The King's Breakfast" (Milne, 1924), in which the King preferred butter with his bread instead of marmalade, set up a tasting table with crackers, wooden spreaders, marmalade, and butter. Children taste each choice, then sign their name under either marmalade or butter. When all have "voted," review who liked which the best. Count the votes to find out which is the favorite of the group.

- Once in a while children can choose their snack or other food. You could arrange for children to register their choices for vanilla or chocolate pudding for their snack, for orange or apple segments for dessert, or for cinnamon or plain graham crackers.

- Children can vote on which story they prefer to hear before lunch.

Calendars

Make large monthly calendars out of large mural or construction paper. Leave large spaces for each day so children can draw/write/dictate what they will do that day or what they did. Special weather days, or the way the clouds look, can be recorded from time to time as well. Keep the completed calendars in a booklet, or find a place to hang them. One teacher hung the calendars on the backs of the cubbies and was amazed at how frequently children talked about the things they had done and enjoyed in the past.

At the end of the year, look over the calendars and reminisce about the past months. Ask each child to think of the event or events she or he enjoyed the most during the year. Then have the children draw/write/dictate their favorite events for a class booklet titled "The History of Our Room."

Writing to Communicate

To help children gain the idea that writing is used to communicate with others, plan ways they can observe and become involved in writing for a purpose.

- Three-year-olds can observe you writing thank-you notes and invitations on charts. Involve them by asking them to write their names on the chart, using scribbles, drawing pictures, or printing their names using invented spelling.

  - Four-year-olds can dictate thank-you notes, news, or invitations and watch you write their words on a chart. Older fours can add notes or their names to the chart.

  - Four-and five-year-olds can draw and write, using invented spelling, on get-well, good-bye, birthday, and other greeting cards for their classmates.

  - Make birthday, get-well, or goodbye books by stapling children's greetings inside a construction paper cover titled "Happy Birthday," "Get Well," or "Good-Bye From Room . . ."

- Have each child make a drawing to put into a book for a child new to the class. Ask children to draw and write about something the new child should know about the group, or to welcome him or her to the center or school. You might divide the group into thirds, with one third drawing and writing about "Our School"; the second group, "What You Should Know"; and the third, "What We Do In Room. . ."

News Boards

A place for children to leave news or messages of importance encourages writing. Younger children can leave pictures illustrating a trip they took or something else of importance to them. Older children, 4- and 5-year-olds, can post news about events in their home and neighborhood, or leave messages for each other.

2.   *Children Will Express Themselves Through Drawing, Painting, and Writing*

When told "just spell it the way it sounds," children will use letters or representations of letters. They will sound out words when encouraged to do so, printing the letters they hear. Their expression will include creative and imaginative writing.

◆   Set aside spaces both inside and outside the room for writing activities. In addition to providing easels for painting and a shelf of blank booklets and markers, use displays and the computer center to encourage writing and establish a writing center.

Create a space for journal writing. A small table and chairs, with a box or other storage arrangement for journals, is all you need. Some centers encourage children to write in their journals any time during the day. Others set aside time for journal writing.

For journal writing to be effective, however, children must have something to write about. To make sure journal writing is productive you might do the following:

• Set aside a table for journal writing so a group of children can talk and share their ideas about an event.

• Make sure journals are handy so children can use them to record special events. One group of four-year-olds took their journals with them when they went outside to observe ducklings hatching from a nest the mother duck had built on their play yard.

• Talk with individual children and ask them to reflect on their day—the things they did, liked, or didn't like—before asking them to write in their journal.

• Ask children to draw/write about

how they felt after a fight

how they feel about themselves

how they feel about other children

◆   Children's imaginations and creativity find expression through drawing and writing. Every day children should spend time drawing and writing. As they do so, they will ask you how to spell words, or ask "Is this right?" Respond by encouraging them to spell the word the way it sounds: "I'll be able to read it." Ask them to think about how the word begins: "Say the word. What sound does it begin with?" Then encourage the child to begin the word with this letter-sound.

Using drawing, painting, and invented spelling, children could write about firsthand experiences, do creative writing, and write stories.

Firsthand Experiences

"TH TRKY WS BG" is the way one child described his Thanksgiving dinner. Use any firsthand experience to spur children's creative writing. You might ask children to write about

• a trip on an airplane

• a storm

• their grandparents' visit

• the trip to the post office, the fire station, a supermarket, a fruit, fish, or green market, or a fast-food restaurant

• what they saw on their walk

• taking apart a clock

• what they did long, long ago when they were babies

Creative Writing

Spur children's creative written expression by asking them to write about

- where their shoes will take them
- what they'll do when they're teenagers
- what would happen if they could fly
- three wishes
- what they see in the clouds
- the story of a blue dragon

Ask children to draw/paint/write

- a picture of the ending of a story you are reading. Compare their endings to the actual ending.
- about their favorite story
- the part of the story that they liked the best, or that frightened or saddened them
- the answer to a question about the story

Compare the children's answers and have the group vote on the one they like the best.

Read a book without showing children the illustrations and ask them to illustrate the story through collage, drawing, and painting.

Story Writing

Children's love of literature spurs them to write their own stories, plays, poems, and rhymes. And when adults begin reading stories with the name of the author and illustrator, it's easy for children to become authors and illustrators themselves.

Use the themes of familiar stories to spark children's creativity.

- After reading *Willie Wonka and the Chocolate Factory* (Bricusse, 1991), ask children to write a story about what they would do if they owned a chocolate factory.
- After reading *And If the Moon Could Talk* (Banks & Hallensleben, 1998), ask children what they think would happen if the sun and stars, clouds, rain, or wind could talk.
- After reading *The Three Bears,* have children write what happened to Goldilocks and the bears after she went home, or after reading *Little Red Riding Hood,* what Little Red Riding Hood and her grandmother did the next day.
- After reading *Julius, the Baby of the World* (Henkes, 1995), ask children to write their own invitation to Julius.
- After reading *The Hunterman and the Crocodile* (Diakite, 1999), ask children to create their own version of this African folktale.
- After reading *Curious George* (Rey, 1973), have children write their own story about Curious George in trouble again.
- After reading *The Complete Book of Flower Fairies* (Barker, 1997), ask children to create their own flower fairy story.

Continue writing pretend fantasy tales. One teacher read a story about the tooth fairy. She asked children to tell who they thought the tooth fairy was: "Are tooth fairies only women? Can they be men? How do they know where to find your tooth? What does he or she do with the teeth?" The children made up their own tooth fairy tales to put in a class book about the tooth fairy.

Many old fantasy tales begin with "Once upon a time." After reading such a folktale, ask children to make up their own story with the beginning "Once upon a time." They need to know that fairy tales are make-believe. Objects, animals, and even the wind and sun have life and can talk and have human traits. Perhaps they could make up fairy tales about

- what would happen if their bikes could take them where the bikes wanted to go

- a rabbit who was their friend

- catching a fish who could talk

- what they would do if they were kings or queens and in charge of the world

3.   *Children Will Contribute to Group Stories and Class Booklets*

◆   Make class booklets revolving around the themes of stories. A group of children could volunteer to create the book, or each child could contribute a page for the book. Children enjoy reading these in school and at home. Some teachers are able to duplicate the booklets so each child can take a copy home; others have children take turns taking the class booklet home with them to share with their parents.

   As a class, children could create their own versions of published books:

- *Brown Bear, Brown Bear What Do You See?* and *Polar Bear, Polar Bear What Do You Hear?* by Bill Martin. Each child could fill a page by writing and illustrating what they hear or see. Or you could duplicate pages for them to complete by filling in the word and illustrating their ideas.

- *Honey, I Love* (Greenfield, 1995). Each child can draw or write about someone or something they love.

- *What a Wonderful World* (Ashley, 1999). Children could draw/write/paint their individual ideas of why this world is wonderful.

- *Amelia Bedelia* (Parish, 1992). How would children extend the idea of Amelia, who literally followed directions ending in disaster, as when she was told to dust the furniture and sprinkled the house with dusting powder?

◆   No story is more loved than the stories of children's own lives.

- Ask children to draw, dictate, or write the story of their life. They can illustrate the story with photographs of themselves.

- Read Bill Martin's *Knots on a Counting Rope* (1969) and have them think ahead. Ask them to write a story about what they will be like and do when they are teenagers, when they are parents, and when they are as old as the man in the story.

◇ Documenting Children's Writing

◆ Begin keeping children's work, either dictated or written, in a portfolio. As with children's progress in printing, collecting samples of the stories and other works they have written lets you clearly see the progress they are making in using story structure and form, in invented spelling, and in the development of their creative and imaginative thought.

◆ Display examples of children's written work so they and others can reflect on the learning experiences of the early childhood program.

◆ From time to time, you can frame children's work to let them know the value you place on their ideas expressed through invented spelling.

◆ A web can both illustrate and document the integrated nature of children's learning to write through invented spelling.

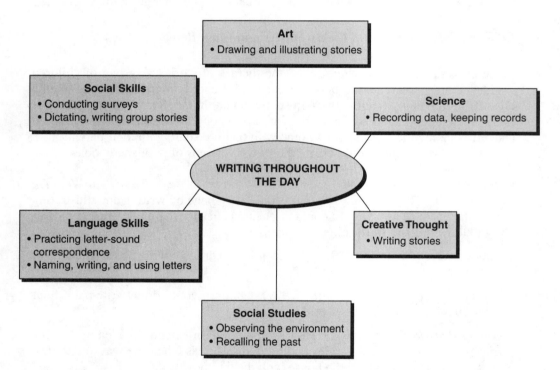

Art
• Drawing and illustrating stories

Social Skills
• Conducting surveys
• Dictating, writing group stories

Science
• Recording data, keeping records

WRITING THROUGHOUT THE DAY

Language Skills
• Practicing letter-sound correspondence
• Naming, writing, and using letters

Creative Thought
• Writing stories

Social Studies
• Observing the environment
• Recalling the past

Date

Dear Families:

Did you know that every day you are teaching your children to write? Every time they see you writing a grocery list, a letter, or in your journal, your children are learning not only that print carries a special message, but how to write themselves.

Engage children in writing with you. You may ask them to sign a birthday card to Grandma or to create a birthday picture or letter. Or ask your children to add items to your shopping list. They might draw a picture of something they want or use invented spelling or "pretend" writing to do so.

Children can also write along with you when you

- write in your journal. Give them a blank book for them to record in drawing or words the things that happened to them during the day and their thoughts.

- work on the computer. They can hunt and peck their names and messages to grandparents, other relatives, and friends.

- address an envelope. They might add their name to the return address.

- fill out a form for school. Let them make check marks in the appropriate boxes and/or sign their names.

Little by little, as children see you writing and participate in writing, they will learn to name letters, learn how to write letters, and learn the sounds of letters.

Sincerely,

8

Second Language Learners
English as a Second Language

FOR THE TEACHER

◇ What You'll Need to Know

Increasingly, our nation is becoming more linguistically and culturally diverse. An estimated one in five children now live in homes in which languages other than English are spoken. In the future this number is expected to increase across the nation. By the year 2010, it is expected that nearly one fifth of the school-age population will be comprised of children whose primary language is other than English (Washington & Andrews, 1999). Additionally, many children will come to the early childhood setting speaking a variety of dialects and will be unfamiliar with standard English used in the classroom.

Historically, early childhood programs have been designed, and even created, to accommodate to the needs of children whose families were new to the United States (Beatty, 1991). The first kindergartens and many child nurseries in this country were developed for the sole purpose of enabling children living in poverty and those from immigrant backgrounds to succeed in the United States.

Today's early childhood teachers, however, have an increased awareness of the need to acknowledge and address the needs of children from linguistically and culturally diverse backgrounds and of the challenges inherent in doing so. Many, faced with the challenges of teaching children from different cultural communities, find research and theory on bilingual education useful.

Based on the theory and research, teachers plan and implement early education programs designed to meet the needs of children and their families who are learning English as a second language.

- They respect (hold in high regard), honor (use children's home language in the early childhood setting), value (esteem, appreciate), and support children's home language and the cultural values and norms of the home (NAEYC, 1995).

- They strengthen parent/school linkages by planning to involve parents in both home and in-school activities (Garcia, 1996; NAEYC, 1995; North Central Regional Educational Laboratory [NCREL], 2000).

- They implement an integrated, thematic curriculum that actively involves children in meaningful experiences. The more meaningful the curriculum, the more deeply embedded within the context of children's lives, the more productive the learning (Dewey, 1944; Garcia, 1996; Vygotsky, 1978).

- They arrange for small group, collaborative, and cooperative learning. Organizing the room and curriculum around centers of interest is one way to promote interaction with others that leads to small group, collaborative work.

- They acknowledge that children can demonstrate their knowledge and capabilities in many ways (NAEYC, 1999).

◇ Concepts Key to Second Language Learning

- Children's home language is deeply respected.

- Linking home and school through language activities is essential.

- Children learn second languages more efficiently when they are able to interact in small groups, and are engaged in meaningful, active experiences that make the need for listening, speaking, writing, and reading real and necessary.

◇ **Goals and Objectives**

Respect will be demonstrated for children's home language.

Home and school will be linked through language learning activities.

Children will develop skills in listening and naming sounds around them; listening to and repeating stories, rhymes, chants, and poems; and listening to each other.

Through active experiences, children will increase their ability to speak, talk, write, and make their ideas, thoughts, wishes, and needs known.

◇ **What You'll Need**

Requirements include

- a wide variety of art and writing materials
- carefully selected children's books that reflect children's home language and culture
- translators who can help you speak and write salient words and phrases in children's and their parents' home languages

Resources

There are numerous resources available for teachers of non-English-speaking children. It may take a bit of searching, but the following offer lesson plans for teaching children and activities for working with parents, as well as position statements, usable theory and research, and the suggestions of teachers and others who have actually taught English as a second language:

National Clearinghouse for Bilingual Education (NCBE)
Center for the Study of Language and Education
George Washington University
2011 Eye St. NW Suite 200
Washington DC 20006

askncbe@ncbe.gwu.ed
www:http://www.ncbe.gwu.ed

National Association for Bilingual Education (NABED)
1220 L St. NW Suite 605
Washington DC 20005-4818

nabe@nabe.org
www:http://www.nabe.org/

National Association for Multicultural Education (NAME)
1511 K St. NW Suite 430
Washington DC 20005

nameorg/@erols.com
www: http//www.inform/umd.edu/NAME/

◇ The Home-School Connection

When working with parents who do not speak English, teachers have found the following practices helpful:

- Take a tour of the community in which the children live. Note resources families could use and those that would be resources for the classroom. You might note a library, fast-food restaurant, play yard, or church.

- Make home visits. To break the ice, take along a book written in the family's home language or samples of children's work.

- Actively involve parents in activities such as Family Nights Out or in the classroom as aides, volunteers, or translators.

- Send home samples of children's work with explanations written in the parents' home language.

- Support children's home language use in the classroom.

- Make certain that signs in the school and room reflect parents' home languages.

- Since you cannot speak every language children will bring to the classroom, enlist parent volunteers, students from a university, or a resource person from a local church to help you learn to understand and speak some essential words.

A "Family Night Out"

Family Night Out was initiated in one school system to introduce parents, most of whom had been born in a country other than the United States, to the curriculum of the childcare program. All parents, however, will enjoy participating in a Family Night Out devoted to language learning.

Family Night Out begins with a dinner in which teachers, children, and their families eat together and enjoy each other's company. After dinner, families circulate through centers of interest designed to involve children and parents. One center could be a hat-making center. Place a chart listing the names of hats children know near a table holding hat-making supplies. All kinds of paper, a stapler, glue and other fasteners, feathers, stickers, buttons, and other hat-making materials can be used by parents and children to make a hat. You could encourage parents to make hats they wore in their home country.

At another center, children and parents have the option of making their children's names in a number of ways. A table labeled "Make Your Name" contains plastic letters, chalkboards and chalk, rubber stamp letters, and markers and paper for children to use to assemble, print, or write their names. Show second language learners how their name looks in both languages.

A third center might be a listening center with recordings of children singing the songs and reciting the poetry they've learned. The selections should include songs and stories from the cultures of the families.

After everyone has had a turn to make a hat and work in the other centers, an aide can lead the children to a quiet place in the room where they'll listen to a story. You can then meet with the parents to describe your language learning program. Explain the goals of the centers. The goal of hat making was to engage children and adults in a problem-solving activity that required using language as well as learning the names of a variety of hats; the goal of printing names was to learn letter names; and the goal of the third center was to develop children's listening abilities. Allow time to answer parents' questions and for discussion.

A "Going to School" Meeting

In one school system, a group of kindergarten teachers held a "Going to School" meeting for parents, most of whom spoke a language other than English. With the help of older children and other community members, they showed slides of a typical school day and described what and how children would be learning when in school. They invited parents to ask questions about school. During the meeting, they translated and talked about the meaning of words like "backpack," "snow day," "PTA," "invented spelling," and so on.

◇ Evaluating and Assessing Children's Developing Language Skills and Knowledge

Children

Observations

While children are working and playing together, take some time to observe children's language abilities. As you observe, ask yourself if children are

- moving from communicating with gestures to

- using gestures and a mixture of home language and English to

- understanding the language of others to

- making their ideas, wants, and needs known by speaking English.

Individual Interviews

Since there will be great individual differences in learning a second language, repeated interviews with individual children should be a productive way of assessing their learning.

Interview children at the beginning of the school year, several months later, and at the end of the year.

Sit with a child and a picture:

- Ask the child to name the things in the picture. Record how many things are named and how many names are given in English. Is the child more frequently naming objects and using English?

- Have the child tell a story about the picture. Record the story and note how many details the child included in the story and how complete the story was. Record the number of English words the child used.

Parents

As your goals are to respect children's home language and involve parents and other family members in children's second language learning, assessment could include a focus on parents. During one month, record

- how many parents visited the classroom. Note how many were non-English speakers.

• the signs in the classroom and school. Record how many of these are in children's home languages.

• how many words you can say and understand in children's home languages.

• your comfort level in working with parents who are non-English speakers.

FOR THE CHILDREN

1. *Children Will Experience Respect for Their Home Language*

◆ If you do not know how to pronounce children's names, ask parents to teach you the correct pronunciation and practice until you reach proficiency.

• Is there a meaning to children's names? Have the tear-out sheet on page 66 written in parents' languages to find out why children were given their names and what the names mean. Or ask parents to tell you the story of children's names so the children can discuss the meaning of their names in class.

   When children bring back the notes, read *How I Named the Baby* (Shute & Grant, 1993), the story of how a family decided on the new baby's name, and discuss how and why the children received their names.

• Make a chart of children's names and their meanings to display in the hall or classroom. Ask children to illustrate the chart with drawings of themselves. Or you could make a class book with a page for each child to draw their picture and print their names if they can. You can record the story of their name.

◆ In some cultures, nicknames hold great importance (Rodriguez, 1999). In Hispanic cultures, nicknames are often better known among Spanish friends than given names. Ask parents if they have special nicknames for their children or terms of endearment. Using their nicknames or terms of endearment lets children know they are loved at home as well as at school and is one way to celebrate the cultures of the children (Rodriguez, 1999).

◆ How do people around the world express their love for children? Hispanics say they have "two handfuls of love" to describe how much they love their children. In France, people call loved ones *petits choux,* "little cabbages." Make a list of the words families use to describe their love. Use these to make a class booklet titled "Love" for Valentine's Day.

How do you say
LOVE:

Two handfuls of

Petits/Choux

my Button

◆ With the help of a translator or parents, go through the school and translate important signs into the languages of the children and their families. Use children's home languages to label things in the room, on charts, and in news letters and other written materials.

2. *Children Will See Their Home and School Linked Through Language Learning Activities*

◆ You might ask parents from various cultures to tell or read folktales from their culture. One mother, a recent immigrant from India, read Demi's *One Grain of Rice*

(1997) to a group of children. Afterward the children tried to count up how many grains of rice they would have if they doubled the number each day.

A mother from Peru read Lois Ehlert's *Moon Rope: A Peruvian Folktale* (1992) to the class. After hearing the story in English and Spanish several times, the children were given metallic pieces of paper precut into geometric forms and other shapes and created their ideas of the Fox, Mole, and other animals trying to reach the moon.

◆ Everyone loves to tell folktales. Ask parents to tell folktales from their cultures. You, in turn, can tell the children folktales from our culture such as *The Three Pigs, Three Billy Goats Gruff, Little Red Riding Hood,* or any others. Then have the children tell their own stories or folktales.

One four-year-old from Russia told of the big fish that everyone wanted to catch. "He fished and fished, but didn't catch me," he said, then continuing, "She fished and fished, but didn't catch me." After he was finished, the children drew and painted pictures of different people trying to catch the big fish that always got away.

◆ Introduce children to music, song, and dance from other cultures. Parents and members of the community might be willing to teach you a few songs, chants, or dances or to teach the children. Many resources, however, are available. Here are just a few suggestions:

Arroz Con Leche: Popular Songs and Rhymes from Latin America (1992), Lulu Delacre

Brown Girl in the Ring: An Anthology of Songs from the Eastern Caribbean (1997), Alan Lomax

De Colores and Other Latin-American Folk Songs for Children (1999), Jose-Luis Orozco

Everybody Sings Freedom (1990), Pete Seeger

Gonna Sing My Head Off! (1995), Kathleen Krull

International Folk Songs: Melody, Line, Chords, and Lyrics (1997), Hal Leonard

3. *Children Will Develop Listening Skills*

They will name sounds around them, listening to and repeating stories, rhymes, chants and poems, and listening to each other.

◆ Children who are just learning language need to be able to hear specific sounds and patterns of their own language as well as English. Specific listening games may be a useful introduction to foster children's ability to listen to the sounds of language. As they listen to and identify sounds, they will also be learning new vocabulary.

• Play "Picture Sounds." This helps children learn to listen to specific sounds as well as to gain vocabulary in both languages. Select a group of pictures that illustrate different sound sources. Mount these on heavy cardboard or construction paper cards and laminate them if possible. Then play the game "Picture Sounds" with a small group of children and a leader. The leader places the cards facedown on a table and asks one of the other children to take a card. The child, without letting anyone see her or his picture, tries to imitate the sound the picture suggests. The other children and adults try to guess what picture the child is holding from the sound she or he makes. Start with animal sounds and machine sounds, and

then move to something more complex, such as the sound of liquid pouring from a glass, the ticking of a clock, the click of a camera, or the whir of an eggbeater.

- Give children a selection of pictures of things that make an assortment of sounds. You will need to cut these pictures from magazines because young children can't handle magazines, scissors, and finding pictures at the same time.

  Three-year-olds will simply paste pictures randomly in their scrapbook. Four-year-olds will be more selective and may group sounds by those they like. Five-year-olds can make booklets titled "Sounds I Like," "Sounds at the Farm," "Sounds I Don't Like," or "Sounds I've Never Heard."

- Arrange a listening station where children can listen to tapes of themselves singing, of the sounds they've recorded on sound walks, or of music, poems, or favorite stories.

4.   *Through Active Experiences Children Will Gain in Their Ability to Speak, Talk, and Write*

◆   The following activity is useful in teaching children names of things in their everyday environment. It was used to help a group of migrant children feel more comfortable in the school environment. Begin by reading the favorite *Brown Bear, Brown Bear What Do You See?* (Martin, 1969). After children are familiar with the refrain, ask them what Brown Bear would see in their room. They may name desks, tables, chairs, easels, blocks, and the things they play with. Increase their vocabulary by asking them if they know the names of other things in the room, the school, or the neighborhood—you may name window blinds, a microwave, fluorescent lights, an overhead projector, or a copier that Brown Bear sees.

Make a list of all the things the children name. Be sure to use both English and the children's language as you do so, obtaining the help of a translator when necessary. Then make a class book naming the things Brown Bear sees in their environment. You could make multiple copies of a page labeled "I see a . . . looking at me" in English and the children's home language. Then each child could fill in the blank with the name of something they think Brown Bear would see in their school or neighborhood and illustrate their ideas. Ask children to try to spell the word, writing it the way they think it sounds. Put all the pages together in a book for the library area called *Brown Bear Sees.* It's great if you have the resources to make copies of the book for each child to take home.

Make the home-school connection. Get a stuffed teddy bear (and name it Brown Bear), a carrying sack, a bound notebook, and a paperback copy of the book *Brown Bear, Brown Bear What Do You See?* Send the bear, notebook, and book home with each child in turn in the carrying sack. Each child then writes in the notebook what Brown Bear saw in his or her home and returns the sack the next day, telling the others what Brown Bear saw and choosing the next child who will take Brown Bear home.

◆   For children learning a second language, singing and chanting rhymes and poems as a part of a group build their confidence in their ability to listen and to speak another language. There's a measure of safety when you are just one among many speakers. In a group, you can practice pronouncing strange words; if you mispronounce a word, no one knows. And singing in a group gives everyone the chance to feel that they belong and are safe and secure.

A wide range of songs, poetry, and chants are available from every culture.

- Say and chant nursery rhymes together.

- Play "In a Spider's Web," a Japanese game, different versions of which are found in many cultures.

Sing or chant

> In a spider's web, one elephant was hung.
> She was lonely there, so she called another one to come.
> In a spider's web, two elephants were hung.
> They were lonely there, so they called another one to come.

As you chant, one child, playing the elephant, wanders around the room. She or he picks another child to be the second elephant. Continue the game until all children are in the spider's web.

- Chant the repetitive phrases of familiar stories. Peregoy and Boyle (1993) encourage the use of patterned books, books characterized by the repetition of phrases, refrains, and rhymes. These help children with limited second language fluency to expand their command of English vocabulary. Using oversized patterned books with groups of children seems to engage second language learners in practicing English (Peregoy & Boyle, 1993). For example, if reading Slobodkin's *Caps for Sale,* stop and have the children recite the phrase "Caps, caps for sale, 50 cents a cap!" Take turns playing the peddler and the monkeys. Select a peddler, who chooses as many children to be monkeys as you have room for. Acting as the narrator, the children repeat the words of the peddler and the monkeys.

  Or read or tell folktales with repetitive phrases. Use the story of *The Three Little Pigs* and have the children repeat the phrase "I'll huff and puff . . . ," or use *The Gingerbread Boy* and have the children repeat "Run, run, as fast as you can . . ."

- Sing "Old McDonald Had a Farm" and have fun exploring the sounds different animals make. Have children make the sounds in English and then in their home language. Listen and compare how people make the same animal sounds in different languages.

- Use finger plays to give children other opportunities to listen and respond with purpose and intent. Playing "Five Little Speckled Frogs," "Two Little Blackbirds," "Five Little Chickadees," and others not only gives children enjoyment, but strengthens their ability to listen and respond meaningfully.

- Ask parents to teach you some of the finger plays they use in their cultures. Learn these and have the non-English-speaking child teach them to the other children.

◆ Plan time alone with children who are learning to speak a second language. Talking, listening, naming things in the child's environment, or repeating phrases is not only meaningful for language learning, but shows respect for each child and his or her culture.

Sometimes it's enough just to sit and chat with a child on a bench or under a tree outside. Other times you might

- engage in picture reading. Together you and the child read a picture. You could point to objects in the picture and talk about them (Hernandez, 1997). Say, "This is a picture of a house. Here are the windows. This is the door," and so on. Ask the child to teach you the names for these things in his or her language. Continue by talking about who might live in the house or what is inside the house.

- read a book together, engaging in dialogical reading. Stop and ask the child to talk about the pictures, to tell what happens next, or to read along with you.

- play a board game. Show and tell the child how to play the game, naming the pieces, the colors, and the parts of the game.

- use a flannel board to tell a familiar story. As you tell the story of *Three Billy Goats Gruff,* the child places the characters on the flannel board. Then switch roles and have the child tell the story and you place the figures on the board.

◆ The most productive times for all children—but especially for those who are just learning language—to learn language, to speak, listen, talk, and make their ideas, thoughts, and wishes and needs known are during center time and at recess.

- When engaging in sociodramatic or any other type of play, children are forced to listen and communicate critically in ways that

    convince each other of their point of view—"You be the baby. I'll be the daddy."

    keep the play moving along—"This is the hose. Put the fire out, shish, shish, shish."

    enable them to solve problems—"Here, you hold this, and I'll put the ladder here. Then the house will stand."

- Project work engages children in listening to and analyzing the messages of others. When children are asked to work together on a project, they must develop the skill of listening critically to one another. Children talk, listen, and use language to negotiate as they work together to

    construct an animal of boxes and found objects

    interview center staff and parents to find out what can be done about the litter around the play yard and then report back to the group

    dig a garden and plant seeds and bulbs

◆ The language experience approach to learning to read and write has been recommended by experts in multilingual language learning (Gunderson, 1991; Hernandez, 1997). Basically this approach is based on three ideas:

- You can talk about the things you have experienced.

- What you talk about can be written.

- Writing can be read.

People recommend the language experience approach because it "capitalizes on children's linguistic, cultural, and social strengths while matching their interests and concerns, background knowledge, and language proficiency" (Hernandez, 1997, p. 172).

Begin with an experience shared by the group. It may be taking a walking field trip, blowing milkweed seeds in the wind, raking leaves, walking on a sandy beach, or something as simple as watching a spider climb up a wall. Once children have experienced something together, they have something to talk about.

The experience of a group of four-year-olds consisting mainly of Hispanics who were learning English illustrates how the language experience works to promote speaking, listening, reading, and writing. In this group, a study of trees led to a study of wood. After a trip to buy wood and supplies, the children learned to hammer nails into the wood. They hammered and hammered. When they were finished, the teacher asked them to tell *how* they hammered. Each child, including those who were just learning English, described, in words and motions, how she or he managed to hammer nails in the wood. The words the children used were written on a chart in English and Spanish. When children didn't know the word to express how hard or carefully they hit a nail, new vocabulary was introduced and the words written on a chart.

Next, the children were asked to draw themselves hammering. Consulting photos taken while they had hammered, the children drew themselves and wrote, using invented spelling and scribbles, how they hammered.

To conclude the language experience, the children were encouraged to "read" their stories to each other. A class booklet of pictures and stories in both English and Spanish was placed in the library area. Children read and reread the book and told over and over again exactly how they hammered nails into boards.

◇ Summary

Clearly, teaching children English as a second language is a challenge—yet a challenge that teachers have successfully met by developing deep respect for children's home languages, arranging the classroom in ways that permit children to use both their home language and English as they interact with others, and implementing a developmentally appropriate curriculum.

Children develop listening and speaking skills as they take part in the activities of the early childhood program. As they use one another's names, listen to American folktales and those of their native country, and sing and chant songs and poems together, they develop skills in listening to and speaking English.

As children take part in meaningful experiences, they will use both languages to express their ideas, feelings, and knowledge. They will learn that what they experience can be talked about, and what they say can be drawn or written and then read by others.

Throughout the curriculum, carefully foster the comfort and security necessary to learn a second language. Use children's home language in print and speech. Note and meet children's language needs individually. And give each individual whatever time she or he requires to develop mastery over their first language at the same time they are gaining mastery over the use of English.

◇ Documenting Children's Second Language Learning

◆ Keep portfolios. Begin a portfolio on each child with records of the observations you've completed and individual interviews. Collect samples of children's art and other written work. From time to time, you could include photos of the children interacting with each other or of some other language achievement.

◆   Make a web to document how children learn a second language in your classroom.

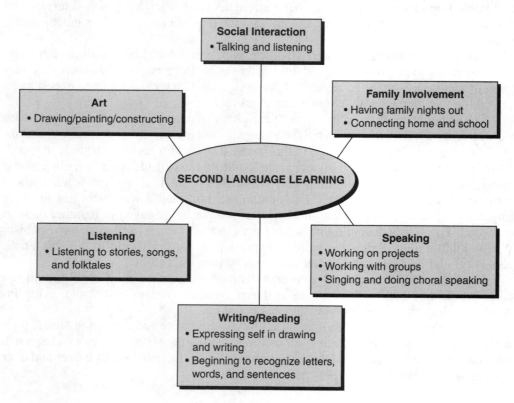

References

Adams, M. J. (1998). *Beginning to read: Thinking and learning about print.* Cambridge, MA: The MIT Press.

Applebee, A. N. (1978). *The child's concept of story.* Chicago: University of Chicago Press.

Beatty, B. (1991). *Preschool education in America.* New Haven: Yale University Press.

Berk, L. E., & Winsler, A. (1995). *Scaffolding children's learning: Vygotsky and early childhood education.* Washington, DC: National Association for the Education of Young Children.

Blaska, J. K., & Lynch, E. C. (1998). Is everyone included? Using children's literature to facilitate the understanding of disabilities. *Young Children, 53*(2), 36–40.

Bredekamp, S., & Copple, C. (1997). *Developmentally appropriate practice in early childhood programs* (rev. ed.). Washington, DC: National Association for the Education of Young Children.

Bredekamp, S., & Rosegrant, T. (1995). *Reaching potentials: Transforming early childhood curriculum and assessment* (Vol. II). Washington, DC: National Association for the Education of Young Children.

Bronson, M. B. (1995). *The right stuff.* Washington, DC: National Association for the Education of Young Children.

Bruner, J. (1966). *The ecology of human development: Experiments by nature and design.* Cambridge, MA: Harvard University Press.

Bruner, J. (1966). *Toward a theory of instruction.* Cambridge, MA: Belknap/Harvard.

Byrne, B., & Fielding-Barnsley, R. (1993). Evaluation of a program to teach phonemic awareness to young children. *Journal of Educational Psychology, 58,* 488–503.

Byrne, B., & Fielding-Barnsley, R. (1995). Evaluation of a program to teach phonemic awareness to young children: A 2- and 3-year-old follow-up and a new preschool trail. *Journal of Educational Psychology, 87,* 141–151.

Castle, J. M., Riach, J., & Nicholson, T. (1994). Getting off to a better start in reading and spelling: The effects of phonemic awareness instruction within a whole language program. *Journal of Educational Psychology, 86,* 350–359.

Chomsky, N. (1986). *Knowledge of language: Its nature, origin and use.* New York: Praeger.

Clay, M. M. (1979). *The early detection of reading difficulties* (3rd ed.). Portsmouth, NH: Heinemann.

Cummins, J. (1989). Empowering minority students: A framework for intervention. *Harvard Educational Review, 56,* 18–35.

Dewey, J. (1899). *School and society.* Chicago: University of Chicago Press.

Dewey, J. (1938). *Experiences and education.* New York: Collier Books.

Dewey, J. (1944). *Democracy and education.* New York: The Free Press.

Dighe, J., Calomiris, Z., & Van Zutphen, C. (1998). Nurturing the language of art in children. *Young Children, 53*(1), 4–9.

Downing, J. (1973). *Comparative reading.* New York: Macmillan.

Dyson, A. H. (1993). *Social worlds of children learning to write in an urban primary school.* New York: Teachers College Press.

Ermi, L. C., & Wilce, L. S. (1987). Does learning to spell help beginners learn to read words? *Reading Research Quarterly, 22,* 47–65.

Gambrells, L. B., & Mazzoni, S. A. (1999). Emergent literacy: What research reveals about learning to read. In C. Seefeldt (Ed.), *The early childhood curriculum: Current findings in theory and practice* (pp. 106–133). New York: Teachers College Press.

Garcia, E. (1996). *The education of linguistically and culturally diverse students: Effective instructional practices.* Santa Cruz, CA: National Center for Research on Cultural Diversity and Second Language Learning.

Genishi, C., & Fassler, R. (1999). Oral language in the early childhood classroom: Building on diverse foundations. In C. Seefeldt (Ed.), *The early childhood curriculum: Current findings in theory and practice* (pp. 54–80). New York: Teachers College Press.

Gesell, A., Ilg, F., & Ames, L. B. (1974). *Infant and child in the culture of today.* New York: Harper & Row.

Gonzalez, V. (1996). Theoretical and practical implications of assessing cognitive and language development in bilingual children. *Bilingual Research Journal, 20*(1), 93–131.

Goodman, K., & Goodman, Y. (1989). *The whole language evaluation book.* New York: Heinemann Educational Books.

Grolnick, W. S., & Slowiaczek, M. L. (1994). Parents' involvement in children's schooling: A multi-dimensional conceptualization and motivational model. *Child Development, 65,* 227–252.

Gunderson, L. (1991). *ESL literacy instruction: A guideline to theory and practice.* Upper Saddle River, NJ: Regents/Prentice Hall.

Hernandez, H. (1997). *Teaching in multilingual classrooms: A teacher's guide to context, process, and content.* Upper Saddle River, NJ: Merrill/Prentice Hall.

Honigman, R. D., & Bhavnagri, N. P. (1998). Painting with scissors: Art education beyond production. *Childhood Education, 74,* 205–212.

Jalongo, M. R. (1992). *Early childhood language arts.* Boston: Allyn & Bacon.

Lanser, S., & McDonnell, L. (1991). Creating quality curriculum yet not buying out the store. *Young Children, 47*(2), 24–29.

Loughlin, C., & Martin, M. D. (1987). *Supporting literacy: Developing effective learning environments.* New York: Teachers College Press.

Mallory, B. L., & New, R. S. (1994). *Diversity & developmentally appropriate practices: Challenges to early childhood education.* New York: Teachers College Press.

Marcon, R. (1992). Differential effects of three preschool models on inner-city 4-year-olds. *Early Childhood Research Quarterly, 7,* 517–530.

Martin, B. (1965). *Sounds of the storyteller* (teacher's ed.). New York: Holt, Rinehart & Winston.

Maryland State Department of Education (1992). *Laying the foundation for school success: Recommendations for improving early learning programs.* Baltimore, MD: Author.

Marzoff, D. P., & DeLoache, J. S. (1994). Transfer in young children's understanding of spatial representations. *Child Development, 29,* 739–752.

Mason, J. (1980). When do children begin to read? An explanation of four-year-old children's word reading competencies. *Reading Research Quarterly, 15,* 203–327.

Mayfield, M. L., & Ollila, L. O. (1998). Parents and teachers: Partners in emerging literacy. In Ollila, L. O., & Mayfield, M. L. (Eds.), *Emerging literacy: Preschool, kindergarten, and primary grades* (pp. 253–279). Boston: Allyn & Bacon.

McKeown, M. G., Beck, I. L., Omanson, R. C., & Pople, M. T. (1985). Some effects of the nature and frequency of vocabulary instruction on the knowledge and use of words. *Reading Research Quarterly, 20,* 522–535.

Moore, C., Angelopoulos, M., & Bennett, P. (1999). Word learning in the context of referential and salience clues. *Developmental Psychology, 35*(1), 60–68.

Morrow, R. D. (1991). What's in an Asian name: In particular a Southeast Asian name? *Young Children, 44*(6), 21–25.

National Association for the Education of Young Children. (1995). *NAEYC position statement: Responding to linguistic and cultural diversity—Recommendations for effective early childhood education.* Washington, DC: Author.

National Association for the Education of Young Children and the International Reading Association. (1998). A joint position statement by NAEYC and the International Reading Association. Learning to read and write: Developmentally appropriate practices for young children. *Young Children, 53*(4), 30–46.

National Council for the Social Studies. (1998). *Curriculum standards for social studies: Expectations of excellence.* Washington, DC: Author.

Neuman, S., Copple, C., & Bredekamp, S. (1999). *Learning to read and write: Developmentally appropriate practices for young children.* Washington, DC: National Association for the Education of Young Children.

New, R. (1999). An integrated early childhood curriculum: Moving from the what and the how to the why. In C. Seefeldt (Ed.), *The early childhood curriculum: Current findings in theory and practice* (pp. 265–289). New York: Teachers College Press.

North Central Regional Educational Laboratory. (2000). *Critical issues: Meeting the diverse needs of young children.* Oak Brook, IL: Author.

Novick, R. (2000). Supporting early literacy development: Doing things with words in the real world. *Childhood Education, 76,* 70–75.

Oates, E. H., & Koelsch, M. (1995). *Making music: 6 instruments you can create.* New York: Harpercrest.

Peregoy, S. F., & Boyle, O. F. (1993). *Reading, writing and learning in ESL.* White Plains, NY: Addison Wesley Longman.

Piaget, J. (1970). *Science of education and the psychology of the child.* New York: Viking Compass Book.

Piaget, J., & Inhelder, B. (1969). *The psychology of the child.* New York: Basic Books.

Powell, D. R. (1989). Families and early childhood programs. *Research Monographs of the National Association for the Education of Young Children, 3.*

Raines, S., & Canady, R. J. (1990). *The whole language kindergarten.* New York: Teachers College Press.

Rivkin, M. (1995). *The great outdoors: Restoring children's right to play outside.* Washington, DC: National Association for the Education of Young Children.

Rodriguez, G. G. (1999). *Raising neustros ninos in a bicultural world.* New York: Fireside Books.

Schickedanz, J. A. (1999). *Much more than the ABCs: The early stages of reading and writing.* Washington, DC: National Association for the Education of Young Children.

Seefeldt, C. (1993). Learning for freedom. *Young Children, 48*(3), 39–45.

Seefeldt, C. (1995). Art—A serious work. *Young Children, 50*(3), 39–45.

Seefeldt, C. (1997). *Social studies for the preschool/primary child.* Upper Saddle River, NJ: Merrill/Prentice Hall.

Seefeldt, C., & Barbour, N. (1998). *The early childhood curriculum: An introduction* (4th ed.). Upper Saddle River, NJ: Merrill/Prentice Hall.

Stahl, S. A., McKenna, M. C., & Pagnucco, J. R. (1995). The effects of whole-language instruction: An update and a reappraisal. *Educational Psychologist, 29,* 175–185.

Stevenson, D. L., & Baker, D. P. (1987). The family-school relations and the child's school performance. *Child Development, 58,* 1348–1357.

Stone, S. J., & Glascott, K. (1998). The affective side of science instruction. *Childhood Education, 74,* 102–107.

Tompkins, G. E. (1996). *Language arts* (4th ed.). Upper Saddle River, NJ: Merrill/Prentice Hall.

Vygotsky, L. (1978). *Thought and language.* Cambridge, MA: The MIT Press.

Vygotsky, L. (1986). *Thought and language* (rev. ed.). Cambridge, MA: The MIT Press.

Washington, V., & Andrews, J. D. (1999). *Children of 2010.* Washington, DC: National Association for the Education of Young Children.

Whitehurst, G. J., & Lonigan, C. J. (1998). Child development and emergent literacy. *Child Development, 69,* 848–872.

Wong-Fillmore, L. (1991). When learning a second language means losing the first. *Early Childhood Research Quarterly, 6,* 323–346.

Wright, J. L., & Shade, D. D. (1994). *Young children: Active learners in a technological age.* Washington, DC: National Association for the Education of Young Children.

Children's Books

Aardema, V. (1998). *Borrequita and the coyote: A tale from Ayutla, Mexico.* New York: Dragonfly.

Ada, A. (1997). *Gathering the sun: An alphabet in Spanish and English.* New York: Lothrop, Lee & Shepard.

Alexander, M. (1998). *A you're adorable.* Cambridge, MA: Candlewick Press.

Ashley, A. (1999). *What a wonderful world.* New York: Chariot Victor Press.

Bang, M. (1980). *The grey lady and the strawberry snatcher.* New York: Four Winds.

Banks, K., & Hallensleben, G. (1998). *And if the moon could talk.* New York: Farrar Strauss.

Barker, C. (1997). *The complete book of the flower fairies.* New York: Frederick Wame Co.

Barton, B. (1990). *Building a house.* New York: Mulberry Books.

Blair, S. (1987). *Three Billy goats gruff: A Norwegian folktale.* New York: Scholastic.

Bond, F. (1985). *If you give a mouse a cookie.* New York: Harper Collins.

Bond, F. (1991). *If you give a moose a muffin.* New York: Nameroff.

Brenner, B., & Chardiet, B. (1993). *Where's that insect?* New York: Cathedral Books.

Bricusse. (1991). *Willie Wonka and the chocolate factory.* New York: Hal Leonard.

Browne, P. A. (1996). *A gaggle of geese: The collective names of the animal kingdom.* New York: Atheneum.

Bryan, A. (1997). *ABC of African American poetry.* New York: Atheneum.

Carle, E. (1974). *All about Arthur.* New York: Franklin Watts.

Carle, E. (1995). *The very busy spider.* New York: Philomel Books.

Carle, E. (1996). *The grouchy ladybug.* New York: Harper.

Delacre, L. (1992). *Arroz con leche: Popular songs and rhymes from Latin America.* New York: Scholastic.

Demi (1997). *One grain of rice.* New York: Scholastic.

dePaola, T. (1978). *Pancakes for breakfast.* New York: Harcourt Brace Jovanovich.

Diakite, B. W. (1997). *The hunterman and the crocodile.* New York: Scholastic.

Ehlert, L. (1992). *Moon rope: A Peruvian folktale.* New York: Harcourt & Brace.

Eichenberg, F. (1952). *Ape in a cape.* New York: Holt.

Feelings, M., & Feelings, T. (1974). *Jambo means hello! Swahili alphabet book.* New York: Dial Press.

Field, E. (1904). *Poems of childhood.* New York: Charles E. Scribner's Sons.

Fleming, D. (1991). *In the tall, tall grass.* New York: Henry Holt.

Freeman, D. (1968). *Corduroy.* New York: Viking.

Gag, W. (1997). *The ABC bunny.* New York: Paper Star.

Greenaway, K. (1886). *A apple pie.* New York: Frederick Warne & Co.

Greenfield, A. (1995). *Honey, I love.* New York: Harper.

Haley, G. E. (1971). *A story, a story.* New York: Aladdin Paperbacks.

Henkes, K. (1995). *Julius, the baby of the world.* New York: Mulberry Books.

Heo, Y. (1994). *One afternoon.* New York: Orchard.

Hoban, T. (1982). *A. B. See!* Chicago: Greenwillow Press.

Hughes, L. (1994). *The collected poems of Langston Hughes.* New York: Vintage.

Hutchins, P. (1971). *Changes.* New York: Macmillan.

Jordan, M. (1996). *Amazon alphabet.* New York: Kingfisher Books.

Kellog, S. (1987). *Aster aardvark's alphabet adventures.* New York: Morrow.

Kraus, R. (1989). *The carrot seed.* New York: Harper Trophy.

Krull, K. (1995). *Gonna sing my head off!* New York: Knopf.

Lear, E. (1999). *An Edward Lear nonsense alphabet.* New York: Harper.

Leonard, H. (1997). *International folk songs: Melody, line, chords, and lyrics.* New York: Hal Leonard Publishing Co.

Lester, H. (1988). *Tacky the penguin.* New York: Houghton/Mifflin.

Lomax, A. (1997). *Brown girl in the ring: An anthology of songs from the Eastern Caribbean.* New York: Pantheon.

Marks, A. (1977). *Ring-a ring o'roses and a ding, dong bell.* New York: N. S. Books.

Martin, B. (1969). *Brown Bear, brown bear what do you see?* New York: Holt, Rinehart & Winston.

Martin, B. (1969). *Good morning, good night.* New York: Holt, Rinehart & Winston.

Martin, B. (1969). *Knots on a counting rope.* New York: Holt, Rinehart & Winston.

Martin, B. (1991). *Polar bear, polar bear what do you hear?* New York: Holt, Rinehart & Winston.

Martin, B., & Archambault, V. (1989). *Chicka, chicka, boom, boom.* New York: Simon & Schuster.

Merriman, E. (1966). *It doesn't always have to rhyme.* New York: Atheneum.

Milne, A. A. (1924). *When we were very young.* New York: Dutton. (This volume includes the poems "Disobedience" and "The King's Breakfast.")

Milne, A. A. (1995). *Winnie the Pooh's abc.* New York: Dutton Books.

Mosel, A., & Lent, B. (1988). *Tikki Tikki Tembo.* New York: Henry Holt & Company.

Most, B. (1995). *Catbirds and dogfish.* New York: Harcourt & Brace.

Murray, B. (2000). *The Reading Genie.* www.auborn.edu/≈murraba

Orozco, J. L. (1999). *De colores and other Latin-American folk songs for children.* New York: Puffin.

Parish, P. (1992). *Amelia Bedelia.* New York: Enoro Clad Books.

Potter, B. (1987). *Peter rabbit's abc.* New York: Frederick Warne & Co.

Potter, B. (1997). *Peter rabbit.* New York: Frederick Warne & Co.

Potter, B. (1997). *The story of Benjamin bunny.* New York: Frederick Warne & Co.

Pringle, L., & Potter, K. (1997). *Naming the cat.* New York: Walker & Co.

Reiser, L. (1996). *Margaret and Margarita—Margarita Y Margaret.* New York: Mulberry Books.

Rey, H. A. (1973). *Curious George.* New York: Houghlin Mifflin.

Rosen, M. (1992). *How the animals got their colors: Animal myths from around the world.* New York: Harcourt & Brace.

Samson, S. M., & Neel, P. (1994). *Fairy dusters and blazing stars: Exploring wildflowers with children.* New York: Roberts Rinehart Publishers.

Seeger, P. (1990). *Everybody sings freedom.* New York: W. W. Norton.

Sendak, M. (1962). *Alligators all around: An alphabet storybook.* New York: Harper & Row.

Sendak, M. (1988). *Where the wild things are.* New York: Harpercollins Juvenile Books.

Seuss, Dr. (1938). *The 500 hats of Bartholomew Cubbins.* New York: Vanguard.

Seuss, Dr. (1957). *The cat in the hat.* New York: Random House.

Shute, L., & Grant, C. (1993). *How I named the baby.* New York: Albert Whitman & Co.

Silverstein, S. (1974). *Where the sidewalk ends.* New York: Harper & Collins.

Slobodkin, E. (1987). *Caps for sale.* New York: Harper Trophy.

Spier, P. (1997). *Peter Spier's rain.* New York: Doubleday.

Stevenson, R. L. (1905). *A child's garden of verses.* New York: Scribner Sons.

Tallon, R. (1969). *An abc in English and Spanish.* New York: The Lion Press.

Tarsky, S., & Ayliffe, A. (1998). *The busy building book.* New York: Putnam Publishing Group.

Tudor, T. (1954). *A is for Annabelle.* New York: Rand McNally.

Watson, P. (1994). *The market lady and the mango tree.* New York: Tambourine Press.

Williams, S., & Schachat, B. (1996). *Mommy doesn't know my name.* New York: Houghton Mifflin Co.

Index